BREAK THROUGH

Learning to Persevere through the Process

Gladimir Simeon

THE SIMEON GROUP
PUBLISHING
-INSPIRE TO MOVE-

E-book ISBN-13: 978-0-9978748-5-3

E-book ISBN-10: 0-9978748-5-3

Paperback ISBN-13: 978-0-9978748-6-0

Paperback ISBN-10: 0-9978748-6-0

The information presented herein represents the view of the author as of the date of publication. This book is presented for informational purposes only. Due to the rate at which conditions change, the author reserves the right to alter and update his opinions based on new conditions. While every attempt has been made to verify the information in this book, neither the author nor his affiliates/ partners assume any responsibility for errors, inaccuracies, or omissions.

Dedication

To Bishop Henry Fernandez and Pastor Carol Fernandez:
Thank you for believing in me, leading by example, and providing the many opportunities to succeed.

To Mary, Karen, Diana, Anite, and Berta
Your love kept me afloat during the most difficult times of my life. Thank you

To My SOP Family and Professors, Faith Center Family and Men of Valor:
Thank you for your support. You were always a light in my darkest days.

To my family:
You supported me fully even before the vision was fulfilled. Your love is unmatched and always demonstrated through action. Thank you and I love you.

Table of Contents

DEDICATION III

TABLE OF CONTENTS V

PREFACE XI

How did the book come to life? xi

What motivated and inspired me through the process of writing? xi

Why me? xii

Why you? xiii

Why now? xiii

Why this book? xiv

INTRODUCTION XVII

CHAPTER 1: THE POWER OF A MADE-UP MIND 1

Defining Breakthrough 2

The Battlefield Is in the Mind 4

Best Practices: Changing the Mental Conversation 7

Greatness within You 8

Storytime: Abraham Lincoln Failing Forward 9

CHAPTER 1: QUOTES TO LIVE BY- PERSEVERANCE 12

CHAPTER 2: VISION VS. SIGHT 13

Vision vs. Sight 14

The Power of Focus 16

Storytime: More Likely to Succeed 17

Best Practices: Write the Vision Make It Plain..............................*18*

Self-concept: Self-esteem, Self-efficacy, and Self-confidence..................*21*

Best practices: Improving Your Self-concept *23*

CHAPTER 2: QUOTES TO LIVE BY- VISION 26

CHAPTER 3: SELF-DISCOVERY.. **27**

No Purpose No Breakthrough..*27*

The Art of Deception..*28*

Who Are You?..*30*

Storytime: My Personal Journey of Self-discovery...................*31*

Who You Must Become *33*

Your Skills, Talents, and Gifts..*35*

Strengths and Weaknesses..*37*

Best Practices: Personal Development *38*

CHAPTER 3: QUOTES TO LIVE BY- SELF-DISCOVERY 41

CHAPTER 4: FRIENDS FOR THE JOURNEY **43**

Defining Friends...*43*

Common Interests *45*

Current Level vs. Future Level..*46*

Storytime: Veiled Best Friend *48*

Good Friend vs. Dream Killers..*50*

Timing of Friends *51*

Developing a Valued Relationship *53*

Best Practices: Networking..*55*

Best Practices: Mentorship..*56*

CHAPTER 4: QUOTES TO LIVE BY- FRIENDS FOR THE JOURNEY 59

CHAPTER 5: COMMITMENT **61**

Story Time: The Commitment of Nelson Mandela.....................*63*

Self-discipline 65

Best Practices: Improving Self-discipline 66

Contingency Plan 68

Best Practices: Constructing Your Contingency Plan 70

CHAPTER 5: QUOTES TO LIVE BY- COMMITMENT 74

CHAPTER 6: NOTHING IS WASTED **75**

Why Your Past is So Important 77

Growing through Experiences.. 79

The Purpose of Emotions 81

Disappointment, Discouragement, and Despair................... 83

Dealing with Disappointment, Discouragement, and Despair... 85

Best Practices: Staying Out of the Pit................................. 87

CHAPTER 6: QUOTES TO LIVE BY- EMOTIONS 89

CHAPTER 7: THE PATH AHEAD **91**

Storytime: Learning Value the Hard Way 92

Roadwork... 94

Your Roadwork 96

Your Comfort Zone: Complacency...................................... 97

Giants on Your Path 99

Storms on Your Path 1001

Mountains on Your Path 102

CHAPTER 7: QUOTES TO LIVE BY- YOUR PATH....................... 105

CHAPTER 8: YOUR BREAKTHROUGH **107**

Always Breaking Through 108

Your Changed Mind 110

What Success Really Looks Like 111

Handling Your Status Change 113

A Walking Testimony.. 114

Enjoying the Process...116

Your Breakthrough Manifested 118

CHAPTER 8: QUOTES TO LIVE BY- YOUR BREAKTHROUGH...........................121

ABOUT THE AUTHOR **123**

A Call to Purpose 124

Preface

How did the book come to life?

This book came to life during the year 2016. At the time, I didn't really understand what a breakthrough was. I had heard of it but didn't understand what it was or how to experience it myself.

Honestly, I believe everyone desires breakthrough in at least one area in their lives. Maybe it's health, finances, family, career, or academically. But how can they if they don't know what breakthrough even looks like? They could've experienced it and not even know it.

Therefore, I felt it was my duty to define what breakthrough is and how to obtain it. The process of obtaining a breakthrough is difficult but worth it. I believe everyone can attain breakthrough if they can endure the process.

What motivated and inspired me through the process of writing?

Writing this book changed my perspective on what was

actually happening to me. The year 2016 was one of the toughest years for me personally, financially, and in my businesses. This was the time I desperately needed a breakthrough in many areas of my life. What kept me motivated was the valley I was experiencing.

If I could find out what breakthrough is, I could experience it myself. Through research and life experience, I came to the realization that breakthrough is a mental experience. Therefore, if I was not experiencing a breakthrough, it was because my thinking was wrong. I'm learning that the more I changed my perspective, the more things around me changed.

As I was writing, my life began to change. I started experiencing a breakthrough in the different areas of my life. This only happened after my mind shifted to see that what was happening to me was part of the process. My breakthrough is manifesting, but it is entirely up to me how much.

Why me?

It is my purpose to help others through inspiration and teaching. It was not always like this. I used to live a very mediocre, sad, and frustrated life. The shortlist of my frustrations included low self-esteem, depression, failed business, dysfunctional marriage, academic inadequacies, overweight, high blood pressure, and poor personal finance.

I was miserable at work, home, and in social gatherings. I wanted more but didn't know how to get it. Even worse, I didn't think that someone like me would ever obtain happiness and success.

It took support, guidance, and action for me to see a massive change in my life. Now, I live a life providing it to others. All of my businesses allow people to live their best life through support, guidance, and action principles.

Personally, I have experienced a massive change in my health, marriage, and businesses as a result of those principles. I learned to tap into my potential and I am discovering new things about myself daily. As a result, I take on new challenges with curiosity and expectation of success.

Finally, I found happiness and success through discovering my purpose. I was meant to inspire others and empower them to passionately pursue their purpose.

Why you?

You need to read this book because your life, your family, and the lives of others depend on it. Your purpose has more attached to it than your happiness. There are so many others waiting on you to impact the world by living out your full potential.

You are much more than what you have uncovered. Your life has much more to experience than what you have experienced. There is so much untapped joy and fulfillment on your path towards purpose. You were sent to earth to live out this purpose, and by not doing so, you're living a very limited, unsatisfying life.

You need to stop fearing your true potential. Your life in your comfort zone is wasting away daily. And you feel it. That is why you are frustrated, unhappy, and depressed. There is more to this life, and you know it, but you fear chasing it because you might fail.

Don't worry; you will fail—probably many times before you finally succeed—but you will succeed eventually. It is part of the process. All you have to do is persevere through it.

Why now?

You need to read this book now and not later. If you want to change your life, you need to take action now. Success only rewards those who take action. The first step to you living your life to the full is learning how to find your purpose so you can begin living it.

Living your purpose is the foundation of your happiness. The capacity of your life can only be filled with purpose. Anything short of that will result in frustration, sadness, and despair. Without purpose, you will never experience the pure joy of impacting the lives of others for their good. This could be in your immediate family or millions across the globe. No one can live the life for you. Neither can you enjoy the happiness of other who are living their life's purpose.

You have to walk your own path. You have to run your own race. Only you can fulfil your destiny.

Why this book?

I don't lie to you; the road to your purpose is hard. There are many failures, setbacks, and obstacles on your way to actualizing your success. Many books tell you to just meditate your way to the life you want; I say you have to take action to get the life you want. But first, you must learn what to expect on your journey.

The principles are very practical and intentional. I want you to take a hard look in the mirror. Your life is what you make it. It won't just change on its own. If you want to see change, you have to take action in the direction of your purpose. Only then will you begin seeing a breakthrough in your life.

Introduction

There is a saying by world-renown motivational speaker Les Brown: "The graveyard is the richest place on earth, because it is here that you will find all the hopes and dreams that were never fulfilled, the books that were never written, the songs that were never sung, the inventions that were never shared, the cures that were never discovered, all because someone was too afraid to take that first step, keep with the problem, or determined to carry out their dream."

We all want to live happier, healthier, more fulfilling lives. So why do very few of us do? Many of us work jobs that we hate. We are in relationships that could be more passionate. Or live a life where we have the time to spend with loved ones having new experiences. Maybe you wanted to start your own business, go back to school, or write your first book. So, why haven't you?

Personally, I remember why I didn't—I was scared. I chose to live a subpar life because I was scared that I was going to fail. But living my life in a box made me miserable, overweight, and impacted my marriage to the edge of divorce. What frustrated me was that I felt called to do more. In the past, I knew I was called to impact the life of so much more people, but I couldn't envision myself doing what I am doing today.

What I am learning on my journey to fulfilling my life's purpose is that it all starts with changing your belief. Once you change your beliefs, your perspectives change. Once you begin seeing things differently, then your actions will change as a result. For example, if you believe that you can be successful in any situation, then the way you view your problems in life will change—they no longer are problems or impossibilities, but they become processes. Your mindset becomes: all I have to do is go through the process to succeed. Therefore, you begin taking action.

Personally, I believe we all are capable of living a life full of purpose. We can't truly enjoy life outside of our purpose. When we live out our purpose by serving and giving to others, what we receive in return is happiness, fulfillment, and sometimes wealth. Discovering the purpose is part of the journey. Your loved ones are there to help you enjoy your journey towards purpose. But there will be many barriers that you must breakthrough to succeed. The first is leaving your comforts.

In this book, you will learn what breakthrough actually is and how you can attain it. You will learn about the path of self-discovery and purpose. Additionally, you will learn about the purpose of friends and mentors on your journey. Most importantly, you will learn about your biggest enemy and how you will overcome each tactic that is meant to hinder you.

I want you to discover how powerful you really are. There is nothing that can stop you from uncovering your truth and living a life of purpose. If you don't reach your goals, it is only because you stopped. No one, no force, or no enemy can stop you. You are blessed and filled with greatness. Only you can stop you from living your truth.

You have a race to run. There will be obstacles on your path, but you must persevere. Don't be misled to believe that there are overnight successes. If there are, they lose their success just as quick. Your journey is meant to prepare you for success and teaches you how to maintain it. Therefore, run your race.

The person starting the race is not the same person who ends the race. The person at the beginning of the race is excited, passionate, smiling, and positive. The person at the end of the race is sweaty, exhausted, beat down, dehydrated, but jubilant. They have gone through trials and tribulation to get to cross their finish line—they attained their victory. The difference between the two runners is the experience. You can choose to stay at the starting line, or you can persevere until you cross your finish line. But nothing will happen unless you start.

-Be unstoppable

MILE

1

Chapter 1:
The Power of a Made-up Mind

What is breakthrough? First, let's start with what breakthrough isn't. Breakthrough is not just the finish line but every step in the race towards it. The person at the beginning of the race is not the same person that finishes the race. If you have ever run a long-distance race or attempted to push yourself past your own perceived capacity, you know that it is arduous. You have to contend with the many thoughts of doubt, pain, and quitting.

Many professional marathoners talk about the mental battle that goes on in the mind in every race that they run. The 26.2-mile race is grueling and many experience excruciating pain in different parts of their bodies in different parts of the race. It seems like the body is fighting against them during the race. It becomes a race of mental fortitude versus just being a physical race. They could stop at any point in the race but they choose to continue regardless of the pain.

About mile 18, their bodies feel as if it is about to shut itself down. The pain becomes unbearable. Their eyes are burning from the sweat. Their mouth is dry and they feel their legs begin to cramp up. Their shins feel like someone stabbing their legs with every step. And then at the moment, they feel they cannot go any further, they catch their second-wind.

Their body begins to relax. Their breathing becomes easier. The burning in the legs begins to subside. No more laboring, no more pain. An ease overtakes them and they feel like they are riding a bike rather than running. Mile-19 through mile-26 goes smoothly as they approach the finish line. They are met by the applause of those that have no clue at how close the runner came to quitting. The crowd is unaware of physical pain or mental oppression that occurred just miles away. How could they know?

As the runner crosses the finish line, the outside sounds fade out to the amplifying inward sounds. Bent over to catch their breath, their hands are on their knees as they frantically search for the internal voices. But there is nothing there. Just silence. The voices that were telling them to quit are no longer there. They stand up straight as a smile emerges on their face. The runner is victorious over their internal enemy.

Defining Breakthrough

Merriam-Webster defines it as:

- an offensive thrust that penetrates and carries beyond a defensive line in warfare
- an act or instance of breaking through an obstacle (a breakthrough agreement)

- a sudden advance especially in knowledge or technique (a medical breakthrough)
- a person's first notable success (breakthrough novel)

When did the runner have breakthrough? Was it at the finish line? The obvious answer is the finish line before the eyes of a multitude of onlookers. But that answer is wrong. Many people would expect the breakthrough occurred at the finish line because they accomplished the goal. However, I like to argue that they would have never gotten to the finish line without completing mile-1, mile-2, mile-3, etc. Each mile has its own challenge and it became harder and harder to continue as they got closer to the finish line. But it wasn't until they felt that they could not take another step that they had breakthrough. The breakthrough was their second wind. They would have never gotten to their breakthrough if they would have quit at mile-17.

The breakthrough manifested itself as a physical second-wind, but the breakthrough occurred in the mind of the runner before the physical manifestation. After the manifestation, the rest of the race was easier. What was once exhausting became refreshing. What was once toiling became fruitful. But it would have never happened unless it occurred in the mind first.

The runner made up their mind to continue amidst what was going on in them mentally and physically. That determination became the catalyst for his breakthrough. According to the definition, the breakthrough occurred when their determination broke through the negative mental obstacles that were telling them to quit. Breakthrough is the point in your journey when you have battled and finally overcome the mental adversity. At that point, you transition from chasing your goal to your goal pulling you. Things become easier. Your daily routines become second nature, and it seems more like riding a bike than running a race. You realized that it's only a matter of time before you are rewarded for your efforts. This is breakthrough.

Breakthrough doesn't happen on the sidelines. Breakthrough does not come looking for you while you are on your couch watching Netflix. Breakthrough won't come wake you up in the morning as you are sleeping. Breakthrough only occurs in the race after running through physical and mental adversity, insurmountable obstacles, and terrorizing opposition. Your determination will be the only weapon that will defeat anything getting between you and your goals.

The Battlefield Is in the Mind

The battle for your goals transpires in your mind. The mind is your greatest help or your biggest hindrance. Many of us experience the power of the mind. When we are inspired, we move in the directions of our goals. But when we allow negativity to plant seeds in our minds, we stop moving forward. Constantly, we are reminded of our inexperience, shortcomings, and past failures. As a result, we never move forward, and in some cases, retreat back into our safe zone. Far away from our pains but also far away from our goals.

We wouldn't ever think about trying to go after our goals especially after failing in our initial attempts. How could you bare another failure since the first one was so bad? Now that memory haunts us whenever we think about another attempt. Your mind becomes your biggest adversary and begins to stand in the way of you and your dreams. Regardless of your past, you must begin to move forward.

You were built to be an overcomer, not a failure. You weren't built to accomplish your goal. It is your purpose in life.

This is why you were sent here—because your story of overcoming was supposed to inspire someone else to persevere. You were sent here help others accomplish their goals. How can you fulfill your purpose if you never pursue it?

Failure only occurs once you quit. Positively speaking, there are only setups to make another attempt at your dream. Try again regardless of your circumstance because your testimony is meant to encourage others.

In spite of that, your enemy does not want you to believe that you can attempt your goal again. How could you—when it seems like such a large, insurmountable goal? But you can and you will. Your enemy will use deception to keep you from attaining your dream. Your adversary knows that if he can get into your mind, he can control your behavior. He will plant the seeds of doubt and let you water it daily with fear, anxiety, and past failures. Your doubt will grow in your mind. But in reality, the chances of you achieving your dream remain the same—it is possible.

Realize that your opponent's resources are limited and he must be strategic with his attacks. Planting seeds takes less effort than battling you. This is why you are deceived in your mind first. If he can stop you there, he won't have to fight you further down your path. That is why he is there to discourage you first thing in the morning, last thing before you fall asleep, and everything in between.

The truth is, your enemy is limited. That is why if you can outlast him in battle, you can defeat him. Persevering is the only way to victory—ask any runner. You will be under attack. But if you endure, you will breakthrough the enemy's attack. Then the manifestation of victory is only a matter of time.

Sun Tzu, the author of the *Art of War*, claims that the

supreme art of war is to subdue the enemy without fighting. Thus, the constant attack on your mind. The enemy knows that if you are determined, there is nothing that could stop you. In other words, once you made up your mind to persevere, no matter what happens, there is nothing impossible for you to accomplish.

Honestly, every successful person had something to overcome. If you hear their stories, you will hear a consensus of how they had to overcome in their minds first. They had to defeat depression in their minds first before they had any success. They conquered low self-esteem and self-confidence in their minds first before their actions changed. They broke the back of rejection in their minds first before going on to achieve their greatness.

If it is possible for them, then it is possible for you. But you must first believe that it is possible. The belief that it is possible is called hope. Hope is needed on the journey towards your goals. It will be the light that shines in the darkness of doubt. The road towards your goals will be lonely and dark but believing it is possible will light the path before you. The more you believe it is possible, the brighter your light will shine.

At first, it will be just a glow, but with each step you take towards your goals, the more you begin to believe. Your hope fuels your action and your action fuels your hope. The corresponding action of your hope is called faith. Faith is an action word. You cannot say you have faith in what you believe in if you never take a step towards your goal. You cannot say you believe you can do it if you are not doing it.

To sum it up, faith is the step forward down the path towards your goals. Hope lights the path before every step. Yet, perseverance keeps you on the path when internal and external forces try to keep you from going down the path.

Best Practices: Changing the Mental Conversation

The first step to defeating your opponent is changing the conversation in your head. Thus far, you have taken everything the enemy has said as truth. But the truth is that you can achieve anything you set your mind to. Therefore, you have to convince yourself that the enemy lies and everything he has said about you is a lie too.

Once you have come to this realization, you have nothing but the truth to stand on. Truth is unshakable and everlasting. The truth is the concrete beneath your feet down the path towards your goal. The enemy wants you to believe that if you walk your path, it will crumble before you; that you will fail as a result, and everyone will see. Stop believing the lie.

You have to stand on the truth if you are going to begin to walk in faith. Knowing the truth about your purpose will set you free from the condemning lies. Change your mental dialogue by aligning it with your truth.

Truthfully, your enemy can't stop you, but he wants you to believe that he can. He will remind you of your failures, your shortcomings, and embarrassments—all in an effort to keep you from taking a step. He will continue planting the same doubts, but you have to be prepared to reject them.

The first step in successful combat is rejecting the lie. Reject them as soon as they come in your mind. Secondly, remind yourself of the truth. Every lie told to you must be quickly replaced with the truth.

Initially, to begin developing your belief in your truth, you have to begin telling yourself the truth aloud. This is called affirmation. Your positive affirmations must be repeated to yourself constantly. Every time the enemy attacks your mind with a negative thought, you counterattack with an affirmation. For example, the enemy says, "You are weak and you will never reach your goals"; you respond with "I am strong and I will reach my goal no matter what." Don't just disagree with the lie; always combat the lie with truth.

You cannot allow the seed of a doubt to fall and take root within your mind. No negative thought must go unchallenged. Fight every negative thought with everything in you. Otherwise, you will never discover the untapped potential that has been lying dormant within you.

Greatness within You

There is greatness within you. This is truth. Why do you think the enemy fights you so hard? He knows that if you were to ever discover your greatness, there would be nothing that could stop you. Once you begin walking in faith, it would only be a matter of time before you were to succeed.

Your enemy wants you to believe that the odds are stacked against you and you won't defeat him. The truth is, you are destined to win if you remain in the fight until the end. You can't quit. You will win if you continue to walk in faith down the path of truth towards your goals. The road won't be easy. There will be setbacks, but that doesn't change your truth.

There is a misconception that failure is final. Failure is not final but the next step in your success process. You cannot obtain success without failing at anything. There are many lessons in failure that you might never have learned if you would have succeeded. Likewise, there are many things about yourself you would never have learned without failure. Determination, perseverance, grit isn't developed when you're constantly winning. Unless there is resistance, there is no growth. Indeed, how could you determine you are an overcomer without ever having to overcome anything?

Without adversity, you will never encounter your greatness. The resistance is meant to draw out your truth. It forces your inner-overcomer to reveal itself to you. Many of us would find this out if we didn't quit after our first failed attempt. But we allow fear to keep us from our greatness. Fear is a lie. Fear makes you believe the worst about your situation—lies about how you can't change your circumstance. It is easy to fall into the trap of believing that the goal is unattainable, but you must be steadfast in your thinking.

Don't allow fear to dictate your behavior. Focusing on fear can paralyze you and keep you from working your faith out. Many people on the sidelines of life have allowed the fear of failure to remain in their thought-life. But it's only through faith that greatness will be revealed.

Many of our most successful leaders encountered some type of failure. Nonetheless, it was only through determination they prospered. Now their stories are told to inspire others.

Storytime: Abraham Lincoln Failing Forward

Abraham Lincoln became the 16th President of the United States of America in March of 1861. However, it's not common knowledge the road that he took to the presidency. What we may remember from our history classes is that he was elected after failed attempts, freed the slaves, and then was assassinated. Little is told about his exceptional leadership during one of the bloodiest wars in American history.

His story goes much deeper than that. It was a 30-year journey through many valleys before he reached his mountain of success. Through numerous failures, he endured on his way to the presidency. Below, I listed the failures and setbacks of Abraham

Lincoln. What amazed me about his story is that even after each failure he would chase bigger goals, never wavering from his ultimate vision for himself.

From 1832 to 1839, Abraham Lincoln lost his job, was defeated for state legislature (1832), failed in business (1833), lost his fiancé (1835), had a nervous breakdown (1836), and was defeated for Illinois Speaker of the House (1838).

But after every setback, he continued to move forward. In the same time frame, he succeeded in being elected Illinois state legislature (1834), was re-elected Illinois state legislature (1836), received license to practice law (1836), became law partner to John T. Stuart (1837), was chosen presidential elector by first Whig convention (1839).

Some notable failures from 1840 to 1860 were: he was defeated for nomination for Congress (1843), lost renomination (1848), defeated for U.S. Senate (1854), defeated for nomination for Vice President (1856), and again defeated for U.S. Senate (1858).

However, his most notable victories in the same time frame were: elected to Congress (1846), started new law practice with Stephen T. Logan (1841), admitted to practice law in the Supreme Court (1849), elected president of United States (1860).

Abraham Lincoln showed great resolve in the face of all the setbacks. He could have stopped anywhere along his journey, but he kept his vision of his future. He was relentless in the pursuit of his vision. He desperately wanted to become the president of the United States and would not stop until he achieved it.

What vision do you have for your future? Are you passionately pursuing it with everything you have? Or are you allowing your setbacks to stop you?

You can fulfill your destiny too, but you must have a vision of your purpose. The vision of your future is what is going to draw you. But your vision must be clear. Don't allow the 'how' you will get to it stop you. The 'how' isn't important initially. Beginning the journey is the most important part. The 'how' will reveal itself with each step of the journey. Allow your vision for your future to inspire you. The more you focus on it, the clearer it will become. Not having clarity leaves room for doubt to creep in. Don't allow that to happen. Be clear on your purpose. Be clear about your vision.

Chapter 1: Quotes to Live by Perseverance

"Great works are performed not by strength but by perseverance."
— Samuel Johnson

"Breakthroughs happen when limiting thoughts and behaviors are challenged." —Fabienne Fredrickson

"To breakthrough your performance, you must breakthrough your psychology." —Jensen Siaw

"The more you feel like giving up, the closer you are to breakthrough." —Bryan Hutchinson

"The LORD said, 'If as one people speaking the same language they have begun to do this, then nothing they plan to do will be impossible for them!'" —Genesis 11:6

MILE

2

Chapter 2: Vision vs. Sight

For you to walk your path, you need to have a target to strive for. This target is called vision. Vision is a thought or picture of your goal in your mind. Visions have true power. They have the power to pull you into them. At times, it can feel like you were pulled into a movie scene. You can taste, smell, and hear everything going on around you. It feels like you are sitting in the room watching your future-self succeeding.

Because of this, your vision has the power to overwhelm you with emotion. These emotions are necessary because they can fuel you during the good and bad times.

Vision is your truth being played on the movie screen of your mind. It is the glimpse into your possible future. It is only a scene of your potential future. I say potential because we all have the free-will to decide. I don't believe the saying, "Nothing is promised." I believe that there are promises available to all of us.

Similarly, principles are available to all of us. However, we have the choice to use the principle or not. Likewise, our promises are available to us, but we have the choice to pursue them or not.

The promise doesn't change because it is the truth. It won't bend or change for us. The truth always stands unchanged and unmoved. Don't be mistaken; your destiny will never chase you. No prize ever chases the pursuer. You must chase success to obtain it.

However, it is completely up to you if you succeed or not. It is completely up to you if choose to chase it or not. There are no external factors that can stop you. There is nothing in our world that can stop a decision. We give external influences too much power. There are many successful people who have overcome insurmountable odds to achieve their dreams. They chose to chase it.

The person you need to become to attain your vision is much different than your current self. Your future successful self is the person you must grow into. Success always rewards the prepared. The road to success not only prepares you for success but prepares you to keep it.

Vision vs. Sight

Vision is a spiritual invasion of your conscious. It is internal and even though your mind only sees it, your physical senses and emotions can experience it too. The vision can be a one-time occurrence or multiple. But you are left with the memory of the vision. The memory of the vision can be just as powerful as the initial vision. Its purpose is to draw you to it. It will haunt your night dreams and daydreams until you take action. Your vision will only be realized on your path of truth towards your goals. Your vision will never manifest sitting on the sidelines of life. Don't allow fear to paralyze you into inaction. You can either be haunted by regret of inaction or doubt as you are chasing your vision.

On the other side, sight is the physical interpretation of our world with our eyes. Your sight is not always truth because it can be manipulated. If there is any damage to our eyes, it will affect our sight. If there is no light, we cannot see. Moreover, what we see can be controlled by the amount of light available and what it is focused on.

Nevertheless, sight is necessary to navigate our physical world. But it can work against us if we allow it to influence our vision for ourselves. Your current situation is not your ending but your beginning. If you look at your today to determine where you will be in the future, it can be discouraging. Don't give permission for doubt to come in. Allow your vision to encourage you because you know how your story will end.

However, the person you need to become to realize the vision is not who you are today. It is impossible for you to get to your goal with who you are today. Where you are today is a result of who you are today. The only way to change where you are today is by changing who you are. Personally, it amazes me that people move to new cities to escape old problems. But the old problems seem to follow them to the new city too. The problem isn't the city; the problem is that they are still the same person in the new city.

You are your current situation. You are your environment. Therefore, you need to change yourself internally to see an external change. To become the person in your vision will take some personal development (which will be discussed in a later chapter). The person you are today may be fearful, easily discouraged, and unhappy. But your future self is courageous, successful and happy. The road ahead towards your truth will develop into this person.

But if you remain who you are, you will remain where you are. The first step you must take to change yourself is a simple step—write your vision down.

The Power of Focus

There is a common saying that writing your goals down will help you achieve them. When you write them down, you have to be clear on the goal. It cannot be ambiguous or open to interpretation. The more specific the goal, the more likely you will achieve it. The less clear the goal, the less likely you will achieve it. There are limitations on your time, energy, and focus. When you are not clear on your goal, you are aiming your time, energy, and focus in too many directions. Yet, if you have a clear target, you can aim your time, energy, and focus in the direction of the target. Anything that doesn't get you closer to the target can be dismissed as a distraction.

By being clear on your goals, it becomes easier to successfully plan your day with steps toward the goal. But imagine if you are unclear with your goal. One day you are taking action in this direction. The next day your actions are taking you in a totally different direction. No wonder you are not ending up anywhere. Don't be fooled into thinking that movement is progress.

Many people set goals that are very vague and end up frustrated because the movement is not bringing them any closer to their goals. In contrast, those that are very specific with their goals are better able to judge if their efforts are taking them closer or further away from success.

Avoid the frustration by being specific. Imagine describing your goal to a news reporter. You need to answer: who, what, when, where, why. The 'how,' or plan, is not your concern initially. But it will reveal itself on the road towards your goal.

Many people make the mistake of not starting because they do not know the 'how' yet. This is to their own harm. The how will never come looking for them. Rather, the 'how' must be searched for.

The 'how' or plan is only discovered on the road to truth. Reason being that the plan is a process that can only be accomplished in a step-by-step order. All the steps in the plan must be completed before moving on to the next step. You cannot skip any steps. There are no shortcuts. Just lessons that must be learned in order to graduate to the next step in the process. Similar to steps in a staircase. To elevate, you must take it one step at a time. Those who take the overnight success elevator soon find out that they never learned the lessons to keep their success. They usually lose it as quickly as they got it.

Initially, the 'how' or plan may be unclear. But at least plan how you will start your journey and then execute. To effectively navigate towards the vision for your future, you must stay focused. Don't be distracted. Be only concerned with what is in front of you before concerning yourself with the next step.

Storytime: More Likely to Succeed

Moreover, to stay focused on your vision, you must keep it before you at all times. The best way of doing so is writing it down. There was a Harvard study done in 1979 in the Harvard MBA program. In the year of the study, the students in the graduating class were asked, "Have you set clear, written goals for your future and made plans to accomplish them?" There were three different groups that emerged from the study. The first group, which was only 3% of the graduates, had written goals and plans. The second group, which was only 13% of the graduates, had goals, but they were not written down. Lastly, the third group, which was 84% of the graduates, had no specific goals at all.

Then 10 years later, the 1979 Harvard MBA program graduating class participated in a follow-up interview. The comparison of the results of the individual members of each group was surprising. They found that the second group that "had goals but didn't write them down" were earning, on average, twice as much as the third group that "didn't have goals at all." Yet, the first group that had "written goals and plans" were earning on average ten times more than the other 97% in their graduating class.

Now that you know this, how are you going to set goals and plan differently? You are 10 times more likely to succeed if you write your goals and plans down. You must review your goals on a regular basis to make sure that you are taking steps towards them. Keeping them in front of you is important. Hang it up where you will see it every single day to remind yourself. This initial step is crucial to you attaining your breakthrough.

Best Practices: Write the Vision Make It Plain

Goal-setting is a skill that can be learned. To efficiently execute your goal, you have to be very practical in your approach. The best way to do this is answering questions. To find your how, you must first answer why, what, when, where, and who. This will help define the steps necessary for achieving your truth. The simpler the steps in the plan, the more likely it can be completed. The more complex the steps are, the less likely you are going to take the initial step to start. However, overcoming inertia is easy—by breaking down the 'how' into small practical steps.

Firstly, you must begin with a large goal. If it doesn't intimidate you, then it is not large enough. The issue with having a small goal is that when you aim low and then succeed, it does nothing to boost your self-confidence. But if you chose a large goal and then succeed, it skyrockets your self-confidence. Do not get stuck on how you are going attain such a large goal. If you focus on the 'why,' you will find your 'how.' The reason why you want to achieve your goals will be your fuel for finding your how.

Having a distinct why will help you attain any goal. Your why must be compelling enough to get you going not just on the good days but the bad days too. The bad days are a part of the process. Bad days are character-building days. To grow through the process, you need your 'why' to motivate yourself into action. Without having a 'why,' you can be easily distracted and discouraged. But when it gets tough, your 'why' will fuel you forward towards your destiny.

To answer your 'what,' you need to be clear on your goal. What do you want to achieve? The more specific you are, the better. It helps to give your goal a specific number, title, or physical description. For instance, if you are looking to lose weight or increase your income, you need to be very specific about the amount. If you are not specific, you are at risk of setting low, insignificant goals. You will either be unmotivated to chase it or if you attain it, will be unhappy with the results.

Next, you need to answer your 'when' by giving yourself a "lifeline." I like to use the term lifeline rather than deadline because the process of goal attainment is actually giving life to your dream. It is only when you quit that your dream actually dies. Hence the term lifeline should be used to identify your attainment date. Your lifeline can be any amount of time you think you need to achieve your goal. Have a date set for your ultimate goal and for your smaller momentum building goals.

It helps to break your long-term goal into smaller milestones or goals. If your ultimate goal will take a year, you want to break it down into smaller quarterly goals, monthly goals, and weekly goals. This makes chasing your long-term goal easier. As you are conquering these smaller goals, you are gaining "small wins." Small wins help build momentum and boost confidence. Each accomplished small win motivates you to chase the next one on your way to your ultimate goal.

Your 'where' is the place where you will need to go on a daily basis to work on your goal. For some, it may be a gym; for others, it may be Starbucks or a library. But having a 'where' helps you identify the location for your breakthrough. Environment is everything. It can inspire you or discourage you. By choosing the right environment for your work, you can remain focused on obtaining your purpose. This helps you differentiate progress and setback in your mind. Any day you didn't go is a day wasted. For there is no standing still; you are either moving forward or backward.

Find a place where you are inspired to think like others at the next level. Being surrounded by success helps to motivate you to dream bigger. For example, whenever I have large projects to do, I usually drive to our Downtown area. Being downtown motivates me because of the speed and energy in that environment. There are people moving about, chasing their dreams and this motivates me to continue to chase mine. Being around success helps me to realize how attainable it actually is. Eventually, the success becomes less intimidating and more of an expectation.

Your 'where' may be different from mine. But it should be somewhere that will inspire you to think and act like you have already attained your goal. Surround yourself with success and you will become success. Likewise, surround yourself with failure and you will become failure. We are not always fortunate to choose the environments we begin our journey in. But truly knowing yourself distinguishes you from your environment.

In the same respect, to realize your dream, you must be able to see yourself attaining it. The way you see yourself, or self-concept, affects what you will chase. Because internally, it defines your ability to chase and achieve. Yet, self-concept is something that can be learned and developed. Thus, who you are has a direct effect on where you are. Without a strong sense of self, you will be stuck where you are. To change where you are, you need to begin by changing the way you see yourself.

Self-concept: Self-esteem, Self-efficacy, and Self-confidence

Your beliefs dictate your action. This is true for yourself and your situation. For instance, if someone grew up poor and later became a successful entrepreneur earning millions of dollars, they have realized their truth, which is being wealthy. Regardless of where they started, they chose to believe their truth. Thus, the way they view their world is through the eyes of a wealthy person. There are things that a wealthy person does not do because of the way they value themselves. As a result, the way they behave is always aligned with their truth. They only do what wealthy people do, which is limit spending, save, invest. Even if you took their money away from them, they would still believe, perceive, and act according to their truth. They will always find a way to earn the money back and become wealthy again.

On the other hand, if someone was raised in a poor home and they chose to believe that their truth is poverty, their behavior would be much different. The way they would perceive their world would be through the eyes of poverty. As a result, they would act the way someone with poor personal finance would act. Because they believe they should be poor, all their actions must lead them to poverty. Most likely, they will overspend, acquire debt, and have no savings or investments for their future.

What you truly believe about yourself will always manifest in your behavior. It's unlikely that you will act opposed to your beliefs. Talking opposed to your beliefs is easy. But the behavior is always the true test of belief. If you believe you can win, you will always try. If you believe you have the ability to change your world, you will.

According to the book, titled *The Confidence Code* by Katy Kay and Claire Shipman, self-esteem is the belief that you have value in the world. Self-efficacy is your belief in being able to accomplish a specific task. Self-confidence is your belief in yourself being successful in any situation. All three are what make up your self-concept or what you believe about yourself, or your truth.

Someone with high self-esteem understands the truth about their personal worth. They understand that they can have shortcomings but still know they have value. Having high self-efficacy is truly understanding the differences between one's strengths and weaknesses. Highly confident people are more outgoing and willing to take risk because they believe that their truth will overcome any situation.

What makes your beliefs truth is that it is able to withstand the testing. In every situation, your truth will remain the truth. If it changes, it was not the truth. But if it goes through the fire of testing, what comes out is a more refined truth. All the doubts were burned in the fire of trial. Now the truth shines brighter than before.

From our prior example with the successful entrepreneur, if they lose all their money, they will find a way to make it back. But what they also gain is a knowing. They can no longer doubt their truth. Their truth remained even though their money didn't. A knowing is stronger than belief. Knowing is breakthrough. Knowing makes you unstoppable.

The same could be said of giving someone poor millions. They will find a way to lose it all. Most lottery winners go bankrupt within 3 years. They get the money without changing who they are. They never change their beliefs and their poor money management actions manifested as a result. Even after having money, their poverty truth remained.

Self-esteem, self-efficacy, and self-confidence will be tools that you will need on the journey towards your finish line. Unless you cultivate them, they will not be strong enough to endure the battle ahead. At each new stage of your journey, you will be confronted with doubt. Your self-concept must be able to reject it for you to take action and move forward. The following are some best practices in developing your self-concept.

Best practices: Improving Your Self-concept

To increase your self-esteem, self-efficacy, and self-confidence, it will occur outside of your comfort zone. The quickest way to increase your self-concept is to step out and try new things. Only through resistance can anything grow. As you are being challenged, you learn and grow. There will be things you learn about yourself you wouldn't have learned unless you were challenged.

However, if you never step out but continue living your life on the sidelines, you will never grow your self-confidence. Your truth cannot be tested within your comfort zone. You cannot build confidence by only doing the things you have already accomplished. With each new venture, there is more of you that is required to achieve it. Unless you are challenging yourself, you never go further than you have gone or do more than you have ever done.

With each victory, you are gaining confidence. Each adversity is meant to reveal more of your true self to you. As the adversity becomes more intense, it brings out more of your truth. You were called to be great. This requires your challenges to be great to prove your own greatness to you. But you must endure. You are destined to win if you stay in the fight.

The absolute worst thing you can ever do is quit. Personally, I don't think people realize the detrimental impact quitting has on their self-concept. Quitting damages your self-concept. As a result of quitting, you believe that you do not have the ability to succeed. Each time you quit solidifies that belief more in your mind. Your confidence increases and you are less likely to take a chance on another challenge. Soon, trying-setback-quitting evolves into never trying, running from challenges, and then hiding from every challenge. You will remain in your comfort zone unfulfilled and unhappy. You will lie to yourself that you are happy, but truth remains unproven. Thus, you remain unproven.

But when we do step out to do something that we are afraid of, it sparks our inner fire. With each new accomplishment, your confidence about your abilities burns hotter. Don't think that a large step is needed to spark confidence. Just big enough to make you nervous. Each small goal should be larger than the last. In doing so, it will take you further out of your comfort zone.

If it makes you nervous, you will need your faith to accomplish it. But if you step out in faith and succeed, you gain confidence. Yet, stepping out in faith and failing garners a lesson. Unfortunately, many of us stop at the point of failure. We never try again to see if what we learned is enough for victory the next time. Within every setback, there is a lesson to succeed. Success is inevitable if you keep trying. Failure is only guaranteed if you quit.

Persevere through the pain of failing. Allow the adversity to draw out your truth. If you quit, you will never give yourself the opportunity to succeed and gain confidence. You have to endure. You have to see what you are made of. You will never know how much you have in you if you don't push yourself to your limit.

Chapter 2: Quotes to Live by
Vision

"Make your vision so clear that your fears become irrelevant" - Anonymous

"If you are working on something exciting that you really care about you don't have to be pushed. The vision pulls you." – Steve Jobs

"Action without vision is passing time. Vision without action is merely a day dream. But vision with action can change the world." – Nelson Mandela

"A man without vision for his future always returns to his past" - Anonymous

"And the LORD answered me, and said, Write the vision, and make it plain upon tables, that he may run that readeth it." – Habakkuk 2:2

```
┌─────────┐
│  MILE   │
│    3    │
└─────────┘
```

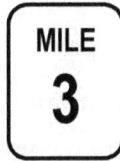

Chapter 3:
Self-discovery

No Purpose No Breakthrough

I have a strong belief that you cannot achieve a breakthrough in your life outside of the path towards your purpose. Many people want breakthrough while they are on the sidelines of life, but breakthrough only occurs in the game. Only in the game of purpose can you obtain victory. Only in the game of purpose will you come against your greatest opposition. Your opponent doesn't want you to win. Your adversary will do everything in their power to prevent you from succeeding.

Regardless of the area in your life that you want a breakthrough, it will be tied to your purpose. Without a greater purpose, there can be no breakthrough. Purpose has to be primary. Unless you are helping others get what they want, you cannot get what you want. If you want success, you have to help others have success first. When you are trying to succeed for your own gains, it won't work for the long term. You may succeed in the short-term, but it's limited in its life and reach.

You will find all that you want in life living in your purpose. To illustrate, if you are being challenged in your health, you can find happiness by encouraging others to continue believing for their healing. As you are persevering and believing for your healing, it will give life and strength to others. It's not only when you find health that inspires others. But the fact that you are in the fight and remain fighting every day. During the good and bad days, you remain steadfast in your truth.

Your personal breakthrough has more to do with others than it does with you. Finding out how you will change the lives of others based on what you have gone through is your task. Once you find that reason, you will find your 'why.' This will be the fuel for you moving forward. Your 'why' is the fire that makes you passionate. You keep your passion by keeping your 'why' burning.

Don't allow what you are going through to dictate how you feel about achieving your truth. Your truth will set you free from your situation if you pursue it. If you believe in your current situation, you are doomed to remain. Don't be deceived.

The Art of Deception

Where you're fighting your greatest challenges may be the source of your purpose. Sun Tzu quotes in the *Art of War,* "All warfare is based on deception. Hence, when we are able to attack, we must seem unable; when using our forces, we must appear inactive; when we are near, we must make the enemy believe we are far away; when far away, we must make him believe we are near." The deception is believing that the area of your difficulties is the area of your weakness, but it isn't.

The truth is, where you're being challenged is the place

where you are your strongest. The fact that you are being challenged in it proves that it is your strength. Your enemy uses problems to deceive you into thinking that it's an area of weakness. Truthfully, the difficulties are there to strengthen those areas. Allow me to explain:

You were sent to this earth with everything that you need to succeed in your purpose. It may be in the rawest form and needs to be developed through knowledge acquisition and trials. The trials are meant to deepen your desire, commitment, skills, etc. The knowledge is meant to articulate the lesson to others to improve their lives.

Essentially, you were trusted with your purpose because you're the only one able to overcome the difficulties associated with your purpose. If you don't get it done, no one can. You are equipped to endure and succeed. You grow as a result of going through the problems. Thus, the trials aren't meant to harm you but to build you. As a result, now you can help others overcome because you overcame.

Your purpose on the earth is to improve the lives of others. How are you making the lives of others better on a daily basis? Perhaps if you were afflicted in your health, you were meant to pray and encourage others to overcome. But first, you must overcome yourself. However, if you quit or decide to live your life on the sidelines, there are others that will be missing out on your story. My favorite book quotes that faith comes by hearing. This is true. Have you ever been encouraged by the story of another person? Their situation may have been worse than what you are facing, but hearing how they endured and overcame encourages you.

Therefore, if you are being attacked in your finances,

perhaps it's your finances that will help a multitude of people. You have heard many stories of millionaires who have come from the worse situations to become wealthy. Their situation is no different than yours other than they chose to believe in their truth and overcame their situation to become successful.

Do not be deceived. You can overcome too. You just need to find your truth, and the truth will free you from the bondage of doubt. When you overcome in your relationships, it will be a testimony to encourage others. But you must endure your circumstances and any challenges that might meet you on your path to helping others out of a troubled situation.

Fundamentally, your purpose is at the core of who you are. Unless you discover who you truly are, you cannot find who you are truly meant to help. Discover your truth by discovering who you really are.

Who Are You?

Who are you? Not many people can answer this question. Most people will answer with their names, titles, or degrees. Those things identify you and give you some type of status. However, defining who you are is defining your truth.

There is a saying that proclaims the two most important days in someone's life is the day that they are born, and the day they discover why. I strongly believe in this. Before you find your purpose, you are alive, but you really aren't living. The day you find your purpose is the day you live on purpose. It is your duty to live out this truth. Essentially, when you are not living your truth, you are living a lie. Lying to yourself leaves you frustrated, depressed, and unfulfilled.

An unfulfilled life is an unhappy life. It is common, but it is not normal. We were meant for so much more. You are special.

You are unique. You are here on purpose. You are not a mistake. All your quirks, shortcomings, and other characteristics make you who you are. They are meant to differentiate you from others because we are not called to help everyone—just certain ones.

Everyone is called to do something different. We all don't possess all the same talents or gifts, but we are all called to use our talents and gifts to help others. If you think about some of the happiest moments in your life, it was when you gave an unexpected gift to someone, or you spontaneously helped someone in need without expecting anything in return. Those moments are when you are tapping into your purpose. Emotionally, it feels good. Sometimes it leaves you happy and energetic the rest of the day.

The same is true for anyone that is fulfilling their purpose on the earth. The people that are the happiest, most energetic, have the best relationships and are positive all the time are the people who are fulfilling their life's purpose. They do not need an alarm in the morning; their purpose wakes them up. There are certain people relying on purposeful people to accomplish their truth that day. Purposeful people realize this and jump out of bed every day ready to live on purpose.

How are you helping others live a better life? Whose life is improved because you got up in the morning and lived your truth? Do you even know what your truth is?

Storytime: My Personal Journey of Self-discovery

Personally, it took me a long time to find my truth. Until I was about 28 years old, I was living a very unfulfilled life. I was depressed, overweight, and my health was in jeopardy. My marriage was in ruin, and I was miserable. The only time I felt happy was when I would encourage others. I loved watching others succeed in reaching their goals—especially as a result of my encouragement or guidance. This was the best feeling in the world for me. However, my job didn't allow me to help others the way I know they needed to be helped.

As a personal trainer, I knew that some of the people that needed the most help weren't getting it in a typical gym setting. Understanding this, I tried my best to coach those who were struggling to lose weight. Though I was not getting paid for the coaching sessions, I felt that this is what I was called to do. But the limits at my job didn't allow me to realize this. Thus, I had a decision to make. Do I live an unhappy but comfortable life, getting paid every two weeks with paid vacation or do I branch out on my own and change the health and fitness industry?

I chose the latter. And it was the scariest and most depressing time of life. But I am grateful that I took the leap and began discovering my truth. If I never branched out on my own, I would never have found who I was called to be. I would never have left my impact on the world. I couldn't imagine going to my grave hiding what was in me. It is a gloomy reality. Can you imagine leaving this earth without a trace of you being here—no impact on others, no legacy to remain after you? This is truly being nobody— to be forgotten.

It is said that the graveyard is the wealthiest place on the planet because there you will find books and songs that were never written, inventions that were never created, and cures for diseases that were never discovered.

The majority of people are not living their truth. What's alarming is that they believe that living a limited life is normal. They are living life within a "small box." They live in this restricted environment their entire lives, scared to break out of it. They are scared of what they might discover about themselves.

They lie to themselves about being happy in the box. But the thing about lies is that you have to keep them going to hide the truth. For instance, "Now is not a good time ..., a majority of people fail in ..., you are not good enough too..." All lies. You will never know for yourself unless you break out of the box.

In this box, every day is the same as the day before. There are no new experiences and no influence on others. It is a mundane, repetitive existence. They repeat the same day, week, month, and year. The only difference is that they get older each year. Some try to mask the truth by self-medicating. But like lies, you need more of it just to maintain it.

But they are alive and unfulfilled. All they have to do is break out of the box to realize their breakthrough. Realize your truth, and your truth will set you free.

Who You Must Become

Life is about relationship. Allow me to explain: Everyone is sent to the earth with a dream or assignment that they must complete before they die. The destiny of many may depend on the destiny of one person. In other words, you must fulfill your destiny in order for others to fulfill theirs. Thus, relationship is connected to purpose.

There are a group of people who are waiting on you to fulfill your dream by helping them to fulfill theirs. Only through this mutually beneficial relationship can you live a full life. The gifts, talents, and experiences are meant to move others forward into their destiny.

This added pressure makes our dreams seem even more intimidating. It can seem like you are further from your destiny now more than ever. The person you are today seems further than who you see yourself become in your vision. The truth is that you cannot reach your dream being who you currently are.

Who you are now has gotten you to your current position in life. For you to move out of this location and towards your dream, you have to become more. The great thing is that what you need to become more is already within you. Your true self is hidden deep within you and must be drawn out. Unfortunately, it is adversity that draws your truth out.

Have you ever noticed how some people react differently under pressure? Usually, great leaders can stay cool under pressure and can keep others around them calm because of their self-assurance. Yet, there are those that crumble under pressure. These bad leaders usually lash out at others as they are feeling the weight of the situation.

Both leaders in the same situation choose to react differently. What they believe about themselves dictates how they perceive their situation and causes them to behave differently. The good leader has discovered his truth. Good leaders are self-aware and, regardless of their situation, are able to see success through the lens of their truth. They are confident that they will find a way to succeed in any situation because their truth has been proven to them many times before.

In contrast, bad leaders crumble under pressure are unaware of their truth. Their truth was never proven. They don't have a history of success to lean on. They don't believe they will survive their situation. Bad leaders don't know the truth of who they are and what they are capable of. Thus, they react to their circumstances emotionally and not with truth. No lens of truth to see through, no victory can be obtained.

Adversity brings growth. For you to develop into the person in your vision, you have to allow adversity to run its course.

Difficulties will reveal many things to you. They will challenge the way you see yourself. As a result, some things will remain. Some things will be stripped from you. Other things will grow. While others will need to wane. As you grow through the hardship, you will discover skills, talents, and gifts you never knew you possessed.

For this purpose, growing requires you to step out of your comfort zone. Staying within the comfort zone is accepting that all things in your life will remain the same. Your truth must be proven to you for you to believe in it. Once it is proven to you, then you will begin to stand on it. With each new challenge that you overcome, you will build upon your proof—eventually elevating from glory to glory until you have a knowing of truth.

If you want a breakthrough, you cannot remain the same person. Discover who you were meant to be and pursue it. Problems are not fun when you are going through it. However, the growth will be worth it. Allow your growth experiences to unearth the skills, talents, and gifts you were sent here with.

Your Skills, Talents, and Gifts

If we were going to try to explain the difference between a skill, talent, and gift, we would have to give it a hierarchy. The skills would be at the bottom of the pyramid. Talent would make up the next level. Then gifts would make the top level. Finding your purpose in life will require that you understand which ones you possess. To fulfill your purpose will require that you develop all three identifying factors. Everything you need to impact your world you already possess. Learn them and develop them for your breakthrough.

My favorite definition of a skill is defined by Merriam-Webster as a learned power of doing something competently: a developed aptitude or ability. A skill is a learn mental faculty or behavior that is developed through practice over time. Some examples of skills are reading, mathematics, cooking, cleaning, and sales. A skill can also be learned at a job to complete a task. Over time, you will get more proficient at the skill. But a skill is limited on how proficient someone can become at it. Hence, everyone can learn a skill; they may not be great at it, but they are able to complete a necessary task using the skill.

Additionally, Merriam-Webster defines a talent as the natural endowments of a person; a special often athletic, creative, or artistic aptitude. Talent is more individualized, and a person is born with a talent. A talent can be limitless but must be developed to realize it's potential. This means you can always improve a talent. Moreover, a talent can allow you to perform a skill efficiently without prior experience. Also, a talent can allow you to learn a skill quicker than someone without that specific talent.

A gift is considered to be God-given, but Merriam-Webster defines it as a notable capacity, talent, or endowment. Your gift separates you from the crowd and makes room for you. Your gift has more to do with your calling than anything else. Your gift is what is going to draw people to you because these are the people you were sent to impact. Your gift is the special endowment that will allow you to realize your purpose.

For example, there are many preachers in the world, but there are some that are gifted to speak to thousands, tens-of-thousand, or hundreds-of-thousands. Their appeal may be to a specific group just because of who they are. They would not be as gifted trying to be someone else. They must live their truth to impact the group of people they were called to. Some people are gifted in taking complex concepts and breaking it down into easily understandable concepts. While others may be gifted in encouraging people—they just know what to say at the right time to uplift others.

Moreover, there are math teachers that are exceptional at helping students who have trouble with math. But then there are one-on-one tutors that have the same gift but are called to a smaller audience. Your gift may be to a smaller group, but your impact is the same. Your gift is tied to who you are called to. If you were to ask the one-on-one tutor to teach an auditorium full of people, they would most likely struggle. Because they are not gifted in teaching larger groups. But you get them in a room with someone struggling with a subject, and the phenomena will happen.

You cannot realize your purpose without developing your skills, talents, and gifts. They are what separate you from others in the similar purposes because you are called to different groups of people. But all skills, talents, and gifts require development for you to fulfill your purpose successfully.

Strengths and Weaknesses

Your skills, talents, and gifts make up your strengths. Your weaknesses are the aspects of your life that you're not proficient in. It is okay for you to possess both strengths and weaknesses. It is impossible for anyone to be great at everything. Having both strengths and weakness are what make us unique.

You must know the differences between your strengths and weaknesses. Confusing your strengths with your weaknesses will be to your detriment. This happens when you're not honest with yourself. Knowing your strengths and weaknesses are important to getting you to your goals quicker. Spend more time strengthening your strengths by learning, practicing, and applying them to your life. This will ensure that you will grow. Personally, I believe spending too much time strengthening your weaknesses is not the best use of your time.

Weaknesses have limited ability for growth. You will only be able to grow so much in your weaknesses versus your strengths. The time needed to make a weakness into a strength is massive. Your strengths have the potential to grow exponentially, but your weaknesses will only grow incrementally. A better use of your time is investing a majority of it on your strengths than your weaknesses. By focusing solely on your weaknesses, your strengths will stagnate. Fulfilling your purpose will require you maximizing your potential in your strengths, not your weaknesses.

Best practices include applying the 80% of your time improving your strengths and only 20% on weaknesses. Partnering and delegating tasks to others that have strengths where you are weak will help you maximize your time. You can't do everything and should never try to. It's crazy, unrealistic, and unsustainable. Your time, energy, and focus are limited. By only focusing on being the best at what you are best at will allow you to impact the lives of others effectively.

Best Practices: Personal Development

Personal development is a lifelong process that improves and increases knowledge, wisdom, experience of an individual systematically through a multitude of mediums and purposeful relationships. What this means is, to improve in an area of your life, you have to research how to improve it. This may be through books, podcast, videos, webinars, seminars, conference, networking, and mentorship.

Many of the most successful people on the planet laud personal development as the reason they are successful. Many have improved their lives by reading the right books and having the right relationships.

Personally, I have seen my income improve with each book that I have read. Books open doors. This means books change your perception. What you have seen before reading a certain book will change. Where you once saw adversity, you will see an opportunity to change your life. And more importantly, have the knowledge to take advantage of it.

Moreover, I feel that each book reveals you to yourself. Each page is like holding a mirror up to yourself. You get to see what you're capable of vicariously through the life of someone else. What you didn't think was possible for you is now possible because the perception about yourself changed. Usually, the author is someone who has struggled with your same shortcomings and was able to develop them and is now sharing how they did it. If you want to believe things are possible for you in a certain area of your life, you need to research and master the teachings in that area.

For every issue, there is a book with a solution. Honestly, there are no secrets to success. If the principle has any credence, then it will be found in a book.

Begin your personal development journey by reading a book a month. You want to understand the book to the point where you can apply it to your own life. The test that you fully understand what you read is that you're able to teach the principle to someone else. You know you have mastered the principle when you can teach someone else how they can apply the principle to their lives and share how the principle has helped your life.

As long as you have a 'why' and a 'what,' the next question you need to ask is who? Who can help me improve in this area? You can ask someone that is already successful in the area you want to improve to suggest some books to you to read. They will be able to help you decide on books to improve your specific situation. Reason being, you want to avoid wasting time, energy, and focus. Leverage your relationships for your advantage.

But changing your life can impact the most by changing your relationships. Who you know will limit what you know. If you are the smartest or most successful person in your group, you need to find a new group. In the next chapter, I will show you how.

Chapter 3: Quotes to Live by Self-Discovery

"Keep a close watch on yourself and on the teaching. Persist in this, for by so doing you will save both yourself and your hearers." —1 Timothy 4:16

"I was not searching for something or someone … I was searching for me." —Carrie Bradshaw

"Life is an endless process of self-discovery." —James Gardner

"Step into the fire of self-discovery. This fire will not burn you but will burn who you are not." —www.thatonerule.com

"Your purpose in life is to use your gifts and talents to help other people. Your journey in life teaches you how to do that." —Tom Krause

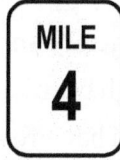

MILE
4

Chapter 4:

Friends for the Journey

Defining Friends

The definition of friendship has changed somewhat since I was a child, or has it? With the advent of the social media, some believe that the meaning of friendship has changed. I beg to differ with that assumption. I believe we all can have a small, intimate group of friends and still have a network of thousands of friends we barely know. Each group has a purpose. The definition of true friends is seen in the inner circle of friends. This group knows who we are as a person. They contribute to the development of who we are as a person in-person.

The other group of friends is on the outer circle of friends. They may not see us in-person, but they do contribute to our development through support through social media, text message, or email. We communicate our thoughts, accomplishments, and challenges with them electronically and they support electronically. Many times, their kind words have more impact on us than people in our inner circle of friends. They provide social proof that our thoughts, accomplishments, and challenges are important. Their care and concern are important to us because they care and are concerned for us.

This proves that what makes people friends is the fact that they are friendly. This is true online and in-person. Both groups are friends, and each has a purpose. In addition, both groups have power. The larger outer circle of friends provides access to a large network of people. With our small group of intimate friends, they can support us in-person, but we are limited to what we can do and accomplish based on who they might know. But with a large network of acquaintances, we can reach out to our network and ask for help. With the latter, who our networks are connected to is limitless—thereby allowing us to be able to accomplish so much more.

Webster's dictionary defines friends as one attached to another by affection or esteem; one that favors or promotes something. Friends are meant to help each other progress based on the affection and esteem they have for each other. An adversary is one who contends with, opposes, or resists; enemy. Thus, an enemy or adversary is meant to stop progress.

The reason that I am spending time defining the differences between a friend and an enemy is that I believe people confuse the two to their own detriment. Most people don't realize who is for them and who is against them until it is too late. However, many of the signs are visible, but you have to be wise enough to look for them.

Common Interests

Most of us choose friends based on common interest. Many of us have friends from childhood that we remain friends with through our adult lives. We remain friends because of shared experiences and shared interest. But once our interest change, we spend less time with each other. As long as all things are common among friends, people remain friends. Yet, once things start changing, there is a possibility that will spend much less time together. This is typically called growing apart.

Things must change within a person if they are expecting their circumstances to change. If things remain the same, you will get more of the same. Likewise, with friendships, as a person desires different circumstances, their friendships must change too. It is much easier getting new friends than trying to change yourself while changing those around you.

Personally, I believe we all have experienced this frustration when trying to improve your friends personally. You try bringing new thoughts and desires into your conversations with them and are met with pushback. For example, when we try to lose weight and encourage our overweight friends to do the same, they get defensive. They are resistant to change and progress in their lives. It is always easier to do nothing but complain about circumstances than put in the effort to change them.

What makes things worse is when your friends try to oppose your progress in subtle but effective ways. Many don't recognize the sabotage until it's too late. In this instance, your inner circle sounds more like enemies than your friends.

What makes them effective is that friends usually know us better than we know ourselves. They know our strengths and weaknesses better than we do—all the things we fail to admit about ourselves. They observed and experienced your shortcoming many times over. They know how committed you are to what you say you are going to do. They know what areas you are weak-willed and not. They know exactly what to say to get you to change your mind about doing the right thing. These same friends/enemies have stood in the way of progress many times than we realize.

Current Level vs. Future Level

It is very true that you are the average of the 5 people you associate with the most. This is true for your finances, weight, education, etc. Like really does attract like. If this principle is true, you are at your current level based on the people that you associate with. If you are to change your life, you must change who you associate with.

I am not saying you should drop your current friends. You can still be friends, but you will hang out with them less for your own benefit. You must take inventory of all your relationships and see what is the benefit of being friends with an individual. Are they adding to you or subtracting? Are they challenging you to improve or sabotaging you? Are they introducing you to new people at the next level or keeping you bound within the group of people you already know?

There is a significant difference between spending time with someone and investing time with someone. The first yields no return, results, or benefits. Essentially, you give your time and get nothing back. After each meeting, you return as the same person as before the meeting. Time is wasted on growth stunting activities that entertain rather than educate. Conversations are spent on critiquing what others are accomplishing rather than their own goals. Time is lost on blaming others for lack of opportunities rather than how to take advantage of present opportunities. You have fun, but you are not growing.

However, investing time with someone always yields results. These meetings are growing your knowledge base or challenging you to be greater. They accelerate your growth rather than stunt it. These encounters provide insight on taking advantage of opportunities. What would have taken years only takes months. Conversations usually revolve around overcoming recent adversities. As a result, you dream bigger because if they succeeded, you can too. You should leave each "investment" meeting empowered and with the knowledge you didn't have before.

These relationships are meant to grow you as a person and progress towards your purposes. This is the true definition of friendship. It's not just having a common interest but how can we benefit each other. Distinguishing the differences between the growth stunting and growth accelerating meetings can be determined in the way you feel once you leave the meeting. Are you energized, motivated, and overwhelmed with the knowledge that you gain? Or are you left feeling drained, demotivated, and comfortable with the mediocracy that surrounds you?

Outward elevation first requires inward elevation. The more you grow, the more you realize how much your friends are not growing. You will try to bring them along but know that you may get pushback. These friends that are resistant to change will keep you bounded in mediocrity. They jeopardize your true potential because they will ensure that you remain the same. The only way you will reach your dreams is by changing your circle.

For you to reach the next level in your potential, you need to surround yourself with people that are that level. Peter Voogd once said, "If you want to become a millionaire, hang with other millionaires. But if you hang with billionaires, you will become a millionaire a lot faster." Likewise, you should choose friends for the journey and mentors as bridges for where you ultimately want to be.

Friends should grow you, not hold you down. Reevaluate who your friends really are. You need friends for where you are going and not where you are. Therefore, choose friends with common ambitions and not because you grew up together.

Storytime: Veiled Best Friend

I have a good friend that I befriended when we were teenagers. We played basketball against each other all the time. He was my fiercest competition and became an enemy on the basketball court. He was also a loudmouth and a ball-hog. But I esteemed him because I valued the confidence he possessed. I didn't realize it then, but some of the qualities that I disliked about him were some of the same qualities I desired for myself.

Being a loudmouth meant he was outspoken, especially when he demanded help to win a game. He was a ball-hog, which meant he never passed the ball, especially when the game was on the line. This meant that he believed in himself enough to always take shots to win the game for him and his team. I realized that I lacked those same qualities and decided to ask for his help and he's been helping me ever since.

He taught me how to shoot a basketball correctly, which eventually got me placed on a high school basketball team. He even got me my first fast-food job after he had been working there himself for several months. He was even the one that trained me on the register and how to serve the food. My good friend even tried to get me another better paying job when he left the fast-food restaurant. Whenever he elevated, he made sure to reach out to me so I could elevate too.

As adults, we matriculated through college. He got internship positions at Fortune 500 companies; he made sure to try to include me. Personally, I never felt like I should take the leap to that next level. I didn't have the confidence and declined all of his offers. But he never stopped reaching out. Eventually, he started his own business and became very successful at the same time I started my failing business. He was becoming more successful, and I was on my second business failure. So, I reached out to him.

He invited me to a party surrounded by his young successful friends. It was very intimidating, to say the least. But at that party, he handed me a book that changed my life. *The Richest Man Who Ever Lived* by Steven K. Scott. This book introduced me to my truth and set me on a course of self-discovery through personal development. Before then, I was too arrogant to admit that I didn't know everything. I would never turn to a book for an answer. After that, I read everything I could get my hands on.

Since then, my friend has reached out to give me book titles that I should read. This one relationship has grown me tremendously. Most importantly, what I learned from him was the difference between a good friend and a bad friend. I did not recognize that he has been my best friend all this time. As he leveled-up, he always made sure that I would too. At first, I couldn't see it. But as a result, it changed my definition of friendship.

We never hung out on a regular basis. I would only see him in-person maybe a couple of times a year. But each encounter, I left more enlightened, empowered, and energized. He was my proof that I would one day capture the goal I was chasing. He inspired me to persevere.

Good Friend vs. Dream Killers

Charlie "Tremendous" Jones was quoted, "You will be the same person in five years as you are today except for the people you meet and the books you read."

The sign that you are growing is discomfort versus the sign of mediocracy is comfort. Be able to recognize the difference between the two. Good friends should make you uncomfortable. Your best friends should always be progressing towards their purposes. You cannot progress in life with people that are willing to live the same day, week, month, year over and over again. You need to pick friends for the journey and not where you are. To achieve success, you need friends with more ambition, vision, and passion than yourself. They will keep you motivated as you are traveling through difficulties.

Feeling uncomfortable around someone you esteem is a good thing. Usually, they are at a higher level that you want to be in yourself. A good friend will see your potential and challenge you to live up to it. This can be very intimidating, but take comfort in the fact that someone believes in you enough to challenge you. They believe that you can achieve your goals if you would just try. They see that you have what it takes to be successful in the endeavor and want to see you attain it. Good friends don't want anything in return for your success and don't want any of the credit. They want you to succeed so they can have good company at the next level.

If you are comfortable with your current group, this is a sign that you are not growing. The chances are that you are repeating the same day over again. No new experiences, books, or relationships. Look at your friends to see your future. Whatever they have, you will have more of the same. If they are not aspiring for anything, neither will you.

Complacency is a destroyer. It is a destroyer of dreams and your soul. You can't ever reach your truth being complacent. In a race, the finish line doesn't come to you. You must run to win. Bad friends will convince you it is safer on the sidelines. Bad friends influence you to give in to fear. They will make fun of the people running their race. They will be there to laugh at them when the runners have setbacks and failures. But they won't pursue their own truth.

Beware of the friends that kill the dreams of others, because they will kill your dreams. Beware of the friends that have no accomplishments, because, by association, neither will you. Beware of people that blame others for their situation, because, by association, you are learning to give away the power to your situation. Beware of friends that don't read empowering books, because, by association, you will be fooled to value all books the same. Beware of friends without new experiences, because, by association, you will live the same day repeatedly. Beware of friends that spend their days talking about others, because they are doing the same to you when you are not around.

In conclusion, you can tell where you are going by your friends. Fulfilling your purpose is dependent on your circle of influence. They can either influence you to persevere or settle-choose wisely.

Timing of Friends

Our lives are seasons that are connected to lead us to our purpose. Each season has different levels within it. Seasons bring new lessons for us to learn to climb to the next level. Every new level is marked by adversity. For us to progress to the next level, we must overcome each challenge. How we overcome each adversity is taught to us in the season.

For example, matriculating through school is similar to seasons and levels. Elementary, middle school and high school would be considered different seasons. Yet, there are different levels or grades within each season or school. Advancement through school depends on if you learn the lessons for that particular level. If you fail at learning the lessons of that level, you will repeat the level. There is a test or adversity at each level to identify if you learned the lessons or not. Thus, no learning equals no advancement.

Moreover, what you learn in elementary school is not what you are learning in high school. However, they are still connected. You must learn the fundamentals before doing more advanced lessons. Therefore, if you are currently in a situation that seems overwhelming, know that you have been prepared to face it. Consequently, if you fail to overcome, know that you will be facing the same challenges over again until you prevail.

Furthermore, as you progress through levels and seasons, your friends change. All relationships have a timeframe. Some relationships, like with your parents, are for a lifetime. Other relationships, like friendships, are for a season in your life. It is rare to have friends for a lifetime, but it does happen. Those relationships need to be honored. Each relationship should be cherished because there are lessons we must learn from each person. This is true for good friends and bad. There are lessons for us to learn in each person that comes into our lives, but it is up to us to learn and then progress forward.

Good and bad friends will be on your journey. Who you chose to befriend and learn from is up to you. Some of your bad friends will have you repeating the same season of your life. Good friends instruct you, encourage you, and hold the door to the next level open for you. But as you matriculate through seasons, you may have to leave good friends behind. When you leave a bad friend, they are fearful that you no longer care about them and will leave them forever. This usually leads to sabotage and other subtle destructive behaviors. Good friends recognize their purpose in your season and are happy to help you achieve your goals. They are usually busy achieving their life purpose to be offended when you leave to pursue yours.

Each season will bring new challenges and new friends to help you through them. Friends should support you as you walking down your path. Challenge you to do more. Encourage you through adversity. In some cases, hold the door open for you at the next level.

If your friends have not done either of the above for you, you need to find a new group of friends. It will be intimidating reaching out to those who are more successful than you. You will be scared. But the worse anyone can say to you is no. But if they say yes, they can introduce you to your next level. The right people will value your ambition and give you their time to see how they can help you. Yet, developing these new relationships determines your future success. Therefore, treat it with that respect.

Developing a Valued Relationship

Developing any relationship should take time. When meeting new people, there is the possibility to meet people that are not genuine. There are people out there that can threaten your success by taking advantage of your inexperience. Therefore, take relationship development slowly.

Personally, I have taken my fair share of lumps. I have lost time, energy, and money getting involved with people that I thought were for me but were only for themselves. But what I gained from each misstep in the relationship process was a new lesson for me the next time I met someone.

Developing a relationship should take time. It is always good to go slow. The successful at the next level will honor you taking your time. The anxious are usually rushing you to your demise. Therefore, take incremental steps in each relationship. Each interaction should move the friendship forward in the direction of each other's dreams.

The relationship should be mutually beneficial. Each partner should be helping the other achieve their truth. Everyone has value and something to offer in each relationship. No one likes to be undervalued. Beware of relationships that only involve how you can help the other person. Even if the other person is at a higher level, you still have a lot to offer. For example, you can provide a fresh perspective which is valuable. A different perspective can provide insight that was not available to the other person.

When you enter a new relationship, you should be asking, "How can I help this person?" Helping others doesn't have to be through your time and talents, but through other relationships, you can leverage. Learning how to connect people with a solution to their problem has tremendous value. This is a skill that will always benefit you. You will be remembered by others as someone that is genuine and willing to help others. This makes you unforgettable. People from the next-level will begin seeking you out and befriending because of this people-centered skill.

As you progress from level to next level, these relationships will be valuable. Thus, treating them different from a typical friendship is necessary. Maintain your esteem and admiration of

Friends for the Journey

each other as long as it is warranted. Learn from each other and grow because of each other.

Best Practices: Networking

Networking is the process of participating in social events to learn how you can help others with their situations. Networking is trying to connect people with people who can solve them. You may have someone in your circle of influence that can help someone you just met at an event. This makes you a problem-solver, even though you indirectly solve other people's problems. This is both beneficial to you and your circle of influence. Your circle gets the referral, and you get to be remembered as a helper. As mentioned before, people remember helpers, and in return, you can get referrals too.

The worst thing to do in a networking function is to go in with the mindset of taking. You must give to receive. But it is when you are going in with a take-mindset that people will avoid you like a disease. No one likes selfish people. Always go to these events with the intent of how you can connect to improve the life of others. You will get back what you give out.

According to Keith Ferrazzi, super-connector and author of *Never Eat Alone*, he mentions always seeking opportunities to network with others. There are many professional organizations that you can join to be part of a like-minded, ambitious group. Find a cause you can be passionate about and join that organization. The best way to meet people is to get involved. Volunteer your time and talents in helping to run a meeting or any special event. To be able to reach more people, run for any volunteer leadership position. This opportunity will lead to you meeting new and interesting people in and out of the organization.

With all new relationships, take your time developing them.

Seek to meet at least one new person at each meeting. Afterwards, try following up with them over coffee. Take your time learning this new person before befriending them. See if they have common ambitions, vision, and passion. In addition, try to find what you can learn from this person. You may find out that they have a solution to your problem.

Follow-up is key. After a face-to-face meeting, you will be able to recognize if the relationship will be mutually beneficial. Those that are not, you can stay connected through social media and quarterly email check-ins. Those valuable connections you can reach out and connect through a combination of professional or social events and group lunches with other like-minded individuals. By connecting, you are helping. The more people you meet, the more your network grows. As a result, the more people you can help.

Remember that these relationships are valuable because they will help you fulfill your purpose. You must be able to recognize if the relationship is helping you fulfill your purpose. Don't waste time with anyone that you wouldn't pay to spend time with. Invest time in those relationships that help you develop and live out your truth. Living your truth necessitates helping others live theirs.

Best Practices: Mentorship

Another great way to improve your life is finding a mentor. Mentorship is the process of partnering with someone with more experience, success, and resources in a particular area for personal, career, spiritual, or relational growth. The mentor has the experience of trying, failing, and eventually achieving their goals. Their wisdom is priceless. It will prevent you from making many costly mistakes. Therefore, seek after and value these relationships.

A mentoring relationship is a delicate relationship that should not be rushed into. You really want to learn the person you want to mentor you because you will adopt the same mannerisms and thought processes. Essentially, they should be who you want to grow into; therefore, character has to be more important than success.

If the person is successful and is a jerk, you too will become successful and not have anyone like or respect you. Their integrity has to be the key thing. Thus, the reason for learning the person over time is important before you commit to a mentoring relationship.

As a mentee, it is important that you act on the advice that is given to you. The mentor has spent years and countless amount of time, energy, and money amassing what they are teaching you. By not acting on the advice is truly disrespectful. No one likes being disrespected.

That is why finding the right mentor is essential to your success. You want to make sure that they have gone through where you are. And they must be where you want to be; otherwise, they won't be able to give you relevant advice. Picking the wrong mentor can leave you with outdated advice or a connection to the wrong network of people for your growth.

Be sure that the mentorship is mutually beneficial. Rarely do mentors want anything in return. According to *Never Eat Alone,* you can honor them by giving your time back to a worthy cause of theirs. In addition, you can help mentor others. What mentors want most is to see you succeed. They take pride in seeing their advice impacting the lives of others.

It is good practice to touch base with your mentor via email to let them know of any wins that their advice garnered. Ask to meet for lunch a few times a year. Moreover, it is good to have different mentors for different aspects of your life, so you don't wear out the relationship with one. Mentorship can be lifelong or for a season. But your genuine gratitude and action are what is going to keep the relationship going.

Mentors and networks can draw your truth out of you. They will challenge your doubts and push you to be greater. They will reassure you when you need to take a leap of faith that you will land eventually. Their stories of overcoming are powerful and help encourage you. Value these relationships and invest time in keeping them because your purpose is tied to them.

Chapter 4: Quotes to Live by Friends for the Journey

"Walk with the wise and become wise, for a companion of fools suffers harm." —Proverbs 13:20

"When you have to start compromising yourself or morals for the people around you, it's time to change the people around you." — Billy Frank Alexander

"Best friends are people who make your problems their problems, just so you don't have to go through it alone." —Anonymous

"Sometimes your circle decreases in size, but increases in value." —Anonymous

"A mentor empowers a person to see a possible future, and believe it can be obtained." —James Hitchcock

MILE

5

Chapter 5: Commitment

Your ability to endure on the road to your purpose is the determining factor to you getting your breakthrough. Earlier, we defined breakthrough as the mental state when you overcome every mental barrier to catch your second-wind for finishing your race. The finish line is not your breakthrough. Actual breakthrough is not public. True breakthrough happens long before others celebrate you for being successful. Breakthrough is the triumph over your biggest enemy—yourself.

For us to persevere to our goals, we first need commitment. Commitment is making up your mind to finish, no matter what. When you commit, you do not stop until you win. You don't stop because you're tired. You don't stop when you're not feeling well. And you definitely don't stop when you experience a setback or defeat. You refuse to lose and don't stop until you succeed.

Truthfully, you are destined to win and fulfill your purpose.

But how many of us endure the hardship, setbacks, defeats, mistakes, and losses until we see victory? Not too many. That is why there is only a small percentage of successful people in the world. It is not that these people had it easy. The successful had to beat insurmountable odds to become successful. Some endured failure and setbacks until they won. Some were labeled as failures from an early age but proved their critics wrong through massive success. Then what makes them different from others who tried and failed? They persevered until they won.

So, why do so many quit? Because it is easy. It is much easier to quit and complain than to endure and succeed. For every one person that succeeded, there are thousands that have tried, quit, and claimed that it was impossible. These people are not committed. Perhaps they expected success to happen overnight. But, with every goal created, there is an equal adversity that is created to test your commitment to your goal.

Why are you being tested? A better question would be: Why not you? If you feel you are destined to fulfill a particular purpose on this earth, PROVE IT. The path towards your goals will through everything at you. Sometimes it's sickness; other times it may be financial issues or family turmoil. If you are truly destined, nothing should be able to stand in your way. If it is the truth, you should be able to prove it against the impossible.

Believing in your truth is one thing; walking out your faith is another. Many people can run their mouths when it comes to what they are going to do. Very few show you through action. Personally, that is why I am never impressed by talkers. I find it annoying. Just show me.

More importantly, show yourself you can do it. Proving it to yourself will cause a bigger mental breakthrough than proving it to others ever will. Do it for yourself, and you will never have to look for others for approval.

Proving it to yourself will take commitment. You will need to find your resolve to endure. Staying resolute should be deeply rooted in your truth. The first step to staying committed is developing your self-discipline. Because without self-discipline, there is no way you can succeed.

Story Time: The Commitment of Nelson Mandela

Nelson Mandela was a South African social justice revolutionary that led a protest against the South African Apartheid. He became the first black president of South Africa in their first democratic election in 1994. He retired in 1999 to pursue other philanthropic endeavors. His most notable achievement was winning the Nobel Peace Prize in 1993. He is admired around the world for his leadership style. He knows when to be firm on certain issues and when to compromise.

Nelson Mandela was the son of a chief of a small South African tribe. His father groomed him for leadership from a young age. He allowed Nelson to sit in on tribal meetings with the elders of the tribe. He went to the best schools and universities available to him in South Africa.

As a young adult, he ran away to Johannesburg to avoid an arranged marriage. Upon his arrival, he experienced the racism of the Apartheid. The Apartheid was established by the National Party (whites only government) who systematically segregated whites from blacks and promoted white privilege. Witnessing the mistreatment of South African blacks, he began a law firm to defend the victims.

He later became the leader of the African National Congress (ANC) who supported a multi-racial democratic system of government. Their goal was to overthrow the government through protest and other non-violent civil disobedient acts. Mandela was arrested on several occasions and was even on tried for treason. This would keep him from being able to leave the country for over four years.

Mandela formed another underground revolutionary group (Spear of the Nation) after the National Party killed 67 men, women, and children during a non-violent demonstration. He realized that non-violent demonstration would no longer work against violent opposition.

Mandela travelled outside of the country raising awareness and support for his cause. When he arrived back into the country, he was arrested for conspiracy to overthrow the government. He was sentenced to life in prison.

Why is he known for his commitment? Nelson Mandela spent 27 years in prison on false allegations of treason. He didn't defend himself in the trial, so as not to give the allegations any credence. He was imprisoned on Robben's Island Prison and forced to do hard labor in a rock quarry.

After his arrest, the cause continued and garnered more momentum. He was seen as a symbol of the injustice that was going on. After 27 years of hard labor, he was released and negotiated the nation's first democratic election.

Nelson Mandela was a committed leader. His why was the equality for all races in South Africa. His commitment cost him two marriages, but he was obsessed with reaching his goal. Even in prison, his passion was able to lead others to continue fighting. I am sure not all his days were good days, but he remained steadfast in his cause. He didn't allow his circumstance to dictate his dedication. He gave up his freedom so that others could be free.

Mandela had vision. He planned for the worst and stuck to his plan. This resulted in his eventual presidency and freedom for an entire nation. What are you willing to sacrifice for your goal? Are you willing to give up your comforts for goal attainment? Will you stay committed in the face of adversity? For you to remain committed will require that you develop in some key areas—the first being self-discipline.

Self-discipline

Self-discipline is the difference between people that are successful and people who are not. Individuals who possess self-discipline can do the things they must do even when they don't feel like doing them. Self-discipline begets consistency. Consistency over time breeds results.

People who are not successful are those that only do what they must do when they feel like doing it. Inconsistent action begets inconsistent or no results.

Can you imagine how much more progress someone would have doing what they need to do day after day? No wonder they are more successful than someone who only does things when it's convenient. For example, if I were to take a step every day for thirty days, I would have taken thirty steps. At the end of a year, 365 steps towards my goal. In contrast, if I were to only take a step when I had free time, or had the energy, or had the motivation to, at the end of thirty days, I would probably have taken just a few steps. At the end of a year, maybe 30 inconsistent steps compared to 365 steps of someone self-disciplined.

That is why self-discipline is the secret to success. Someone that is self-disciplined won't miss opportunities. Regardless if they are motivated or not, they are treating every day as an opportunity to advance. They do what they must do because they realized the significance of every day. An opportunity can present itself at any time. Would you be prepared to take it?

Each day is an opportunity to succeed. Our world is saturated with opportunities to change our lives, but very few of us take advantage of them. Yet, we allow fear, laziness, and ignorance rob us of our opportunities. We all are allotted the same opportunities daily, but only the successful take action. Results come from how you utilize what you're given.

The successful have as many hours in their day as a poor person. But the difference is how each spends their 24 hours. If the unsuccessful wanted to change their situation, they would have to change the way they use their 24 hours. The unsuccessful would only have to consistently do what the rich do, and over time, they will get the same results.

A successful person would wake up early to maximize their day, and then charge their mental, physical, and spiritual battery for the day ahead with a morning routine. Finally, they would attack the day with vigor trying to maximize every minute of their day. They find time to balance work, me-time, and family. They would do this every day without fail.

In contrast, an unsuccessful person would probably sleep-in, start their day watching entertainment television. They spend the rest of the day procrastinating with distractions. They complain about the lack of time and opportunities.

Two different days, two different results. You cannot live the actions of one and not get the results. Therefore, if you do what successful people do, you will have what successful people have.

Best Practices: Improving Self-discipline

Peter Voogd, success coach and best-selling author, mentions that you have to "sell yourself on the importance of doing a particular task." If it is not urgent or important, it doesn't get done. Yet, if something urgent or important needs to get done, you will find a way. Even procrastinators know this. They always find a way to cram to get things done last minute because of urgency and importance.

Selling yourself on the work must be part of your "why." Why is this important for you and your goals? By not selling yourself on the task, you will keep procrastinating with less important tasks.

You're not always going to feel like working but what should motivate you to work is your why. Unless you have a strong and compelling why, you won't have the motivation to get started. Many times we procrastinate on the biggest tasks. These tasks, if done, will make the most significant advancement in our progress.

Don't avoid your biggest tasks; attack them first. In the book Eat That Frog by Brian Tracy, he explains that starting your day with the largest tasks is more efficient than waiting until the end of your day. You have the most energy at the beginning of your day. Therefore, this is the best time to do your most important tasks. Start early to get it done. Get it over with so you don't procrastinate. Tracy explains the principle by using the analogy: If you had a frog to eat each day, the best thing to do is eat it first thing in the morning. By procrastinating, you spend the entire day dreading the task. Eat that frog to get it over with.

Personally, on days unmotivated, I use a timer to hack myself into working. I set a 15-minute timer. If I start working and don't catch a groove in 10 minutes, I will stop and go for a walk and listen to something motivating. But if I do catch a groove, I'll set another alarm and continue working in these 15-minute intervals. Usually, it only takes a couple of times doing this before

I don't need the timers for the rest of the day.

Next, it helps to plan your day better. What helps is planning quiet time to work without distractions. Distractions will kill any momentum you have, especially on those unmotivated days. Sometimes you will need to turn your phone off for a couple of hours as you do most important tasks.

Last but not least, always charge your mental, physical, and spiritual batteries. When you are charged, you will have energy and focus on staying disciplined. This is best done early in the morning before any distractions or responsibilities can get your attention. Begin your morning routine with reading. You should spend 15 minutes reading a spiritual development book, and then invest another 15 minutes in a personal development book. Then you should get 20–30 minutes of exercise. Cardio tends to work best in the morning to energize you the rest of the day. And finally, feed yourself a nutritious breakfast and drink plenty of water throughout the day.

The order isn't important. The most important thing is that you do it. You can actually get all three done at the same time if you listen to audiobooks while you are working out.

This will supercharge your morning and get you ready for any challenges that come up in the day. By not fueling up at the beginning of your day, you make it impossible for you to stay motivated during the ups and downs of your day.

Contingency Plan

Honestly, those who fail to plan really do plan to fail. Therefore, planning and taking appropriate action is necessary for success.

What I have found is that most people do not plan for hardship. They plan their journey optimistically but fail to plan for what can derail them. Challenges are always on the road to success, and you cannot avoid them. It is part of the journey. Adversity is the toll paid to access the road to success.

What ends up happening is that we allow the toll on the road to stop us. Most of us take adversity as a sign to stop. However, the difficulty is a sign to move forward. Difficulty is a sign that you are heading in the right direction. Pay the toll by learning from the challenge and get access to continue down your path towards truth.

Instead, many of us quit and return to our comfort zones. Pay the toll by paying attention to what you should be learning, and then you have access to greater things ahead of you. There is no greatness in your comfort zone. Just pass the toll is the next level for you. Just pass the toll is newer opportunities and experiences. Just pass the toll is fulfillment. Don't give it all up because it's tough.

Personally, I believe that planning for the adversity is important. It is impossible to plan for every possibility. Yet, you can still plan on how you can get around any obvious obstacles. This is called a contingency plan. Contingency plans are implemented when you come against hindrances so that you can remain on the same path. A contingency plan is different from a Plan-B. I don't believe in Plan-B's. Essentially, Plan-B is a way out of a situation or quitting. You are turning away from the original path to find an entirely different path.

A contingency plan is a plan to get back on the road when you do have a setback. Difficulties can be discouraging, and you need something to help encourage you back on the road. Having a contingency plan in place allows you to have a system to manage your challenges, emotions, and focus. You can have a system in place to encourage yourself when you are at your lowest. It's difficult to get back on the road, but you must find a way to stay disciplined.

Personally, part of my emotional contingency plan is taking time out to pray and meditate more. Then I seek the advice of friends, and also make myself available to help encourage someone else. While encouraging others, you come up with the most profound things to say and end up encouraging yourself.

Whatever your contingency plan is, it ensures that there is absolutely no retreat. There is always a way to move forward. You will find a way only if you look for one. The answer can come from anywhere, but you must make yourself available to receive it.

Best Practices: Constructing Your Contingency Plan

Some of the components of a contingency plan are identifying your why, possible issues, self-restart, network restarters.

Your Why: In my opinion, your why is the best place to start from. However, knowing your why isn't enough. You must be so passionate about it that you live it out daily. Be obsessed with achieving your truth. It must penetrate every fiber of your being. Your passion must be so obvious that it motivates others to act. Without your why, any adversity will cool your passion off. Trusting in your why fortifies your confidence in achieving your goals. Your why will keep your passion burning during any obstacles that you may face.

Possible Internal Issues: Next, you must be able to identify potential issues that may arise. These can be internal issues like losing motivation or external issues like running out of resources. Identifying is the first step to preparation. You may not have a solution to every problem, but you want to make sure that you are at least positioning yourself for a solution.

Identifying internal issues requires that you are realistic with yourself. You have to know your strengths and your weaknesses. You have to understand what motivates you and what demotivates you. You have to know who encourages and who discourages. Being honest with yourself is crucial to your success. If you lie to yourself, you're only handicapping yourself. You become your biggest enemy when you're not honest with yourself. To your own harm, you will employ your weaknesses, do the things that demotivate you, spend time with energy-draining people. Don't be surprised when you are not making any progress.

Thus, know thyself. Be honest with the areas you need help in. Know when you work best and how you work best. Know who you work best with and who you don't. Know what makes you go and what causes you to stop. Understand that no one is perfect and even the best of us get demotivated. But the best do have a plan in place to get restarted.

Possible External Issues: Identifying your external issues may be a bit harder, especially if this your first attempt at achieving your goal. You really won't know what to expect. Doing your research is paramount. There is a lot of information online, but knowing how to apply the knowledge to your personal situation is key. Wisdom is knowing how to apply the knowledge. But you want to make sure that you are positioning yourself to receive the wisdom. You want to list mentors or people with experience that you can ask for advice in the particular area. They have gone through what you are in. They will be able to guide you out. Above all, follow the sound advice of your restarters. By not following the advice, you are disrespecting the process by which they acquired the wisdom. The wisdom could have taken them years and heartache to garner, and you want to respect that.

Self-starting: The next step is recognizing what motivates you. This can be listening to music, motivational audios, or watching motivation movies or YouTube videos. Sometimes a change of scenery can spark you into movement.

Also, doing what inspires you can help get you going. Volunteer work or spending time motivating others will inspire you to get back on the road. Encouraging others out of their situation changes the perspective of your situation. People will believe in your belief. If you believe they can make it through, they will believe you. But that entails you believing that you will make it through. Therefore, by encouraging others, you're muscling your way out of a slump.

Network Restarters: The last step is finding those people who can inspire and give you perspective. You can have a few trusted people in this group. This group of people is called your restarters, and you use them to help you to refocus on your goal. They may be able to help you establish a perspective on your situation. It is possible to be too involved in your situation to see a solution. Many times it is right under our noses, and we can't see it. It may be emotion, inexperience, or ignorance that blinds us. But having the right people in restarters group will help maneuver by seeing your blind spots.

Avoid straining the relationship by running to the person with every small issue. Utilize the entire list of people so as not to burden just one person too much. Be sure to choose someone that you respect and value their voice; that way, you are more inclined to follow the advice.

In conclusion, you know the reward is worth the pain. Are you willing to endure the pain for your passion? Will you be willing to test your truth against impossible odds? Commitment is deciding beforehand that you will stay on the path until your dream comes to fruition. If you stay disciplined with your actions daily, you will eventually reach any goals.

Chapter 5: Quotes to Live by Commitment

"Commitment is what transforms a promise into reality." — Abraham Lincoln

"If you want to be taken seriously, be consistent." —Anonymous

"One thing that makes it possible to an optimist is if you have a contingency plan for when all hell breaks loose." —Randy Pausch

"Self-discipline is the bridge between goals and accomplishments." —Jim Rohn

"Grow in self-esteem rooted in being God's workmanship." — Ephesians 2:10

MILE
6

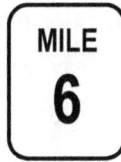

Chapter 6:
Nothing Is Wasted

Nick Vujicic is a world-renown motivational speaker. He has impacted many lives speaking in auditoriums, arenas, YouTube, schools, and universities. He is a loving husband, father, and minister of the gospel of Jesus Christ. He enjoys spending time with his two sons swimming in their pool. Nick is adventurous and loves going to the beach to surf. He has even gone skydiving. He has a Bachelor's Degree in Commerce and is an entrepreneur. He has starred in a short film and won an award for it.

Nick was born with no arms or legs—a condition called Phocomelia. This rare disorder made it hard for Nick growing up. He lived in a home with two loving parents, but it was at school where he was challenged the most. Nick was bullied every day—to the point he was ready to commit suicide at age eight.

Nick's life totally changed when he found his truth in his Christian Faith. He developed a personal relationship with Jesus

Christ, which changed his entire life forever. His personal relationship with Christ has empowered him to live his truth. He lives a life which exceeded his wildest dreams. Now, he speaks to others, sharing his truth, which inspires them to find their truth. Anti-bullying has been his biggest cause for the last several years, and he has been a consultant on national reform.

The question to ask is: How can a man born with no arms or legs accomplish so much? A better question to ask is: How can people born with arms and legs accomplish so little? The short answer is truth. In his past, Nick was depressed to the point of despair. He was ready to end his life. But once he encountered his truth, it changed the trajectory of his life. Before encountering Christ and his truth, he was just existing. Afterwards, he knew why he was born and why he was entrusted to carry his burden/truth.

His burden was Phocomelia. His truth was anti-bullying. His truth has so much impact that on one occasion, during a speech, he was asked for a hug from a girl that was a victim of bullying. He has no arms but gives hugs. He has no legs but has travelled the world and been on stages right before thousands. Out of his lack, the truth is still standing. His truth has withstood so much and is still standing. Against impossible odds, his truth prevailed. He was sent to this earth to fulfill his purpose with the truth locked up on the inside of him.

If he had ended his life at eight years old, thousands of people would not have been impacted by his truth. He was trusted to accomplish his truth on the earth. He was trusted with Phocomelia because only he would be able to endure his path.

We all have been entrusted with a burden for a purpose. But many people stop on their path towards truth because of the difficulty. They were assigned to lead people out of internal and external bondages. They rather settle for mediocrity and blame the burden for their lack. They never step out to discover their truth or assignment. They figure what happened to them was meant to stop them. But the truth is, what happened to you was for your good.

What have you stopped short of in your life? What have you been entrusted with to bring to the world but have kept hidden? What have you looked at as a deficiency or tragedy but was part of your story to inspire others to their truth?

Your truth has the power to withstand anything you have been through so that you can inspire others. You'll never realize who is watching your story. People are always watching. They want to see how you respond to adversity. Consequently, it will determine how they respond to their own. They will persevere because you persevered.

Why Your Past is So Important

By no means am I dismissing the effects of anything traumatic that has happened to you. These negative events are horrible, and no one should have to go through them. They have the power to impact people's lives in a negative way. Some leave wounds that never get the attention needed to heal. This can alter the victim's thinking for the rest of their lives if not treated. But equally as important, what you have been through has the power to help others too.

The negative impact is real. Many times the trauma shapes their personality, mindset, and how they interact with others. The event can distort their belief about themselves, their perception of the world and others, and how they behave.

Most people who have experienced traumatic events are haunted by it daily. Some try to bury the pain under drugs, alcohol, or other negative behaviors. Self-medication is more common than people realize. Because the traumatic event is more common than people realize, they are numbed from the pain temporarily and usually have to continue self-medicating to avoid dealing with it.

Everyone has their burden to carry. Everyone has been appointed with their unique truth. The traumatic event was meant to stop the truth, but you have the power to change that. Your enemy wants you to bury your truth under the hurt, but only you can give your burden purpose. No one can make the decision for you. You have to take that tough initial step of dealing with the trauma.

The traumatic event was meant to bury the truth under pain, shame, self-hate. As a result, rather than fulfilling your purpose, you are wrestling with the issue. We get distracted with the pain such that we avoid finding solutions. The issue gets worse over time and festers into other parts of our lives. Then it seems to be almost impossible to change. We don't believe our truth will ever surface, but it has to.

Rape, molestation, the death of a loved one is difficult to overcome. However, your strength will come from not allowing the traumatic event to define the rest of your life. Some people have overcome such trauma and used it for a greater purpose. They realized that they had been delivered so they can help deliver others. They gain strength and bravery through the event by speaking to others about not stopping where they are. You overcome through action and by testifying to others.

The brave ones inspire others to live their lives, no matter what has happened to them. Brave people have found purpose in their pain. They have accepted their assignment and allowed their truth to shine through the hurt. It takes courage to testify how trauma has impacted your story but not redefined your truth.

Joyce Meyers has turned her traumatic event into a ministry. As a child, she was sexually abused by her father into her teenage years. She was shortly married after her senior year in high school. The marriage only lasted five years, though her husband cheated on her. Shortly after, she met Dave Meyer and soon married. Her marriage with Dave was difficult because of the underlying pain from her childhood.

As Joyce got closer to God, "He began to heal her." He began restoring her and her marriage through Christ and professional counseling. She soon found her passion teaching the gospel of Jesus Christ. She began teaching a Bible class and then started a radio show. She also became associate pastor, and eventually began her own ministry. After some time, she started her own television show to share her testimony. Her truth has impacted millions positively ever since.

Joyce had to deal with what she went through to fulfill her purpose. To fulfill yours will require the help of others. This may be through Christ, counseling, or both.

Growing through Experiences

What are you concealing from the world? What pain are you burying your truth with? What traumatic event are you allowing to dictate your life?

On the path to your purpose, there are many obstacles that you have to transcend. However, it is the intention of your enemy to prevent you from travelling down your road. Sun Tzu quotes, "The supreme art of war is to subdue the enemy without fighting." The trauma was meant to stop you before you ever even started. This is an effective tactic of your enemy. Yet, it is your duty to prevail over anything in your way.

On the path to fulfillment will be many people you were

meant to help. Sometimes you are called to be a friend, give encouragement, lend a helping hand, or give monetarily. Your act is supposed to impact the trajectory of their lives. Yes, we all possess the power to change trajectory, especially with those in our circle of influence.

But if you are not travelling the road, then you are not positively affecting others. You're your past, and don't allow it to haunt you. If you don't, you risk being haunted by the event and reliving the same day over and over again in your mind. The dates on the calendar change but our position in life doesn't. We remain in the place of trauma instead of moving past it.

Being stuck in the same place is painful. Never really living your life to the fullest is a tragedy. Facing your past is the only way to begin the healing process. Without healing, you cannot step into your purpose. Because you have healed, you can show others how to and live their lives to the fullest.

Through healing, a transformation occurs. The trauma is no longer your burden to carry but your symbol of hope. Your story will inspire others to grow through their pain.

The healing process is painful and challenging, but it's worth it. Seeing the impact of your story on the lives of others will inspire you to continue testifying and empowering others. It becomes a reciprocal cycle of inspiration and hope. You're giving out hope and inspiration, and your audience is giving it back to you. Your desire will grow, and you will want to help more people.

Therefore, begin the healing process now and not later. There are so many people waiting on your truth, but you must be willing to uncover many feelings of shame, loneliness, and rejection. And you must fight these demons, not just for you but the benefit of so many others.

Eventually, perspective will change. You will begin seeing your past as your strength and not your weakness. Going through yourself will give you the experience to help others. You will be able to change their perspective about themselves. Your conquest will give your testimony depth and encourage others to pursue their own resolution. Thus, walk it before you can talk it. Doing so will equip you to bless others.

The Purpose of Emotions

Merriam-Webster defines emotion as a conscious mental reaction (as anger or fear) subjectively experienced as strong feeling usually directed toward a specific object and typically accompanied by physiological and behavioral changes in the body. What this means is a feeling that has a physical and behavioral effect on our bodies. There are many different types of emotions. Psychologist Robert Plutchik introduced eight basic emotions that he grouped into four pairs of polar opposites (joy-sadness, anger-fear, trust-distrust, surprise-anticipation), thus creating the Wheel of Emotions. We get all of our different emotions from a combination of these eight basic emotions.

However, to understand the purpose of emotions, you have to look at the etymology or origin of the word. Merriam-Webster claims that emotions originate from Medieval French, from emouvoir to stir up, from Old French esmovoir, from Latin emovēre to remove, displace, from e- + movēre to move. Therefore, the purpose of emotions is to stir us into action. It is very true that your emotions do have the power to inspire you to act.

For example, when I was growing up, there used to be commercials that came on late night, asking for donations to feed the hungry and destitute in a distant part of the world. Many of these non-profit organizations were successful at raising money because the images on the screen were heart-wrenching. Malnourished little kids with swollen bellies and mothers holding their sick children would inspire people to act. Many people picked up their phones and donated.

On the other hand, emotions like fear can keep us from acting too. The fear of rejection, embarrassment, loss, or failure has robbed many people of their dreams. Fear keeps us from growing into our potential. Yet, fear is a choice. It's only real in our minds. What we fear may never happen, but we choose to believe it and remain in our comfort zone.

Indeed, our emotions can be a big asset or a big detriment to our progress. Our emotions will fuel us one way or the other. But taming our emotions is another thing. The more we feed the emotion, the stronger the feeling will be. In other words, the more we focus or think about the emotions, it will amplify and intensify. The only thing that has the power to tame your emotions is an intentional mind.

We have the power to choose to be happy or sad. Honestly, the mind possesses all the power to change our lives. This is only accomplished through intention. The emotions only have the power to amplify and intensify our thoughts so that we act on them, but the mind has the power to harness the emotions. Use your emotions as a tool or your emotions will use you as one.

Personally, I never believed that people cannot control their emotions. Everyone has the power to control their emotions; they just choose not to. For example, people with anger issues are usually able to control their anger in front of a police officer or judge. They just choose not to when they feel like it.

You have the power of choice. If you choose not to use it,

that is your fault. But the power resides in your mind. Your heart is there to help fuel you into action. When you feel you cannot go another step, it is usually your emotions that will push. You have the power. You set the course. Don't allow your emotions to control you.

Disappointment, Discouragement, and Despair

One of the major triggers to us blocking our own success is disappointment. For example, this can be the loss of a loved one, a business client, or your car breaking down. Disappointments are unavoidable. Disappointments are a part of life. Disappointments are like pop quizzes in the curriculum of life. Like pop quizzes, they are unexpected and rarely are you prepared for them. But they will test you. It will reveal what you truly believe.

Some disappointments can be avoided. But, it is impossible to stop all disappointments from forming. Disappointments occur to everyone at every level in life. Negative things are bound to happen; you can't control that. Yet, your response to these occurrences is what you can control.

What makes disappointments so dangerous is the effect that it can have on your emotions. Disappointments can easily turn into discouragement. Discouragement is defined as the act of making something less likely to happen or of making people less likely to do something; a feeling of having lost hope or confidence.

Discouragement is real. We all have had discouragement before. At one point in our life, we all have lost hope or confidence. It feels like we are carrying around an elephant. This weight can keep us from moving forward in any endeavor. We can easily lose motivation to complete the steps necessary for goal attainment.

Discouragement can happen as result of being disappointed

by a person or event. Each disappointment has the goal to impede progress. You can probably think of someone you know that is always discouraging you from chasing your dreams. They are good at listing all the facts why it won't work out for you. They also know the history of other people who have tried it and failed. They warn you about the cost of the venture—and how you will lose time and money that you can't get back.

If you believe them, you have given them power over your emotions. What they are saying is only true in their minds, and they are projecting it on you. They don't know the truth that lies within you, so how can they tell you that what you are destined to do won't work out? Listening to them will keep you in a box destined to get the same-old things forever. You must do new things to get new things.

When discouragement comes from the disappointment of recent events, it will seem to always come at the worse times. Disappointments usually come when you are trying something new. When you finally step out of your comfort zone, there is usually an event to try to scare you back in. The majority of people retreat into their same old life, never to step out again. The retreaters will tell you that it doesn't work. They expected it to be easy.

Many things can trigger distant memories of tragedies or failures. These negative memories keep us focused on our past, thereby keeping us from our future. These triggers act as anchors to our past. Unless we deal with the pain of the memory, we are rooted in our past. Instead of dealing with our past to move forward, we avoid the triggers all together. We will avoid anything that would trigger the memory. Utilizing the action at first seems healthy. But, you are placing yourself in a smaller and smaller box over time.

Avoidance method prevents you from trying new things—just in case the trigger occurs. Thus, you live life a little less each day until your life revolves around avoiding triggers. This is not a life. This is not how you live life to the fullest. Life is meant to live abundantly until it overflows—not less and less until there is nothing left.

Moreover, despair can develop if the disappointment is not dealt with. Despair, defined by Merriam-Webster, means to no longer have any hope or belief that a situation will improve or change. Despair is accepting that things will never improve. You have the power to change your situation. You can get better. Things can turnaround for you. You must believe this if you are going to change it.

Don't get stuck focusing on the situation instead of sticking to your path. Don't have an ongoing pity-party—only discussing the lack in your situation rather than finding an opportunity to change. Things in your life won't change until you make a change. This will take action. This is the only solution to correct your emotional state.

Dealing with Disappointment, Discouragement, and Despair

The ultimate solution is to pick the dream back up and continue to walk forward, regardless of the situation. This is difficult—especially when you don't have any emotional power to stir you up. But you must find a way to get started.

Change always requires action. You cannot wait until you feel better to begin to act. To get out of any emotional pit, you must climb your way out. If you are going to make it out of the pit, you can't wait until you are inspired to act. Unfortunately, despair is digging the pit deeper every day. But making an effort to climb out every day will trigger your hope.

At the bottom of the pit, there isn't much sunlight or hope. The darkness seems endless, and it is easy to lose hope there. At the bottom of the pit, it is easy to drown in despair. Every day you hope for the feeling to leave but without effort to climb out. The hardest climb out is at the bottom of the pit. But it will get easier over time.

As you climb, you will get closer to the sunlight. Your hope increases as a result of the action. The closer you get to the top, the more you want to climb. But, unless you are focused on what is above, your mind will always be stuck in your situation. Keep your mind fixed on getting out. Some days will be harder than others but maintain your focus.

Remember that faith is an action word. It is the corresponding action to what you believe. If you believe things can improve and change, then you have to act like it. Actions say more about what you believe than your mouth ever can.

For those in the pit always say that they want to get out of the pit, but their lack of action say that they desperately want to stay in. You have to make an effort to get out if you ever hope on feeling better. You have to create your own hope through consistent action every day.

As you are climbing to escape, expect that the same issues to come up to try to keep you in. There will be disappointments, discouragements, and triggers as you get closer to the top. Maintain your focus on what is above and don't get distracted with what is beneath you. I admonish you to do what you must to keep climbing out.

Don't be mistaken; the despair will be there to test daily. Many people that have made it out of depression will tell you that the feeling was still there even when things were improving. But they kept climbing out.

They will also testify that even out of the pit, the triggers were there. But they learned to have power over them and not the other way around. They realized that what was happening was trying to distract them from their purpose. Once they made it out of the pit, they didn't make the mistake of staying around it. They began moving down their path to realizing their truth. People that fall back into their pit usually do so by staying around the pit.

Best Practices: Staying Out of the Pit

Move down your path. Staying still will be to your own detriment. You are in danger of falling back into your pit. Don't be satisfied with just getting out of the pit. Make sure that you never fall back into it again by getting as far away from it as possible. This only happens by trying new things.

If you are trying new things, this means that you are growing. What I mean by trying new things is trying new things that will improve yourself. These new things need to grow you as a person of destiny. I don't mean going to a new bar and trying new drinks. Growth is doing the things that you are scared of doing.

You have to fail at something to become better at it. You can't try something new for the first time and expect to be one of the world's best. That doesn't happen. It takes many hours of trying and failing to finally master something. Writer Malcolm Gladwell in his book Outliers claims that it takes 10,000 hours of practice to become world class. The world's best have invested countless hours into becoming the world's best. Becoming good at anything will take time. Don't fear failure but see it as part of the process.

Move forward by trying new things that grow you, even if you don't know what you are doing. You may discover different skills, talents, and gifts you were never aware of.

In conclusion, nothing in your past is ever wasted. It is meant to help you on the road ahead. You can use your negative experience to push you forward and inspire others to move forward too. Or you can give your past the power to keep you bound.

Furthermore, don't allow your feelings to get in the way of your destiny. Instead, use them to fuel your actions.

Chapter 6: Quotes to Live by
Emotions

"Never regret your past. Accept it as the teacher that it is." —
Robert S. Sharma

"A life that is never willing to change is a great tragedy—a wasted life. Change is a necessary part of a growing life, and we need change in order to remain fresh and to keep progressing." —Rick Warren

"You can forget what hurt you in your past; just never forget what it taught you." —Anonymous

"Guard your heart above all else, for it determines the course of your life." —Proverbs 4:23

"If you are going through hell, keep going … you will always grow through what you go through." —Rev Run

MILE

7

Chapter 7:
The Path Ahead

Striving towards your future without dealing with your past is a problem. As stated in the previous chapter, what happened in your past is important to your future. Some people are not able to move forward into their future because they never discovered the purpose of their past. This keeps them from getting closer and moving forward into their destinies. But once you come to the realization that your past can't stop you, then you begin taking steps forward.

The path that is ahead of you is an arduous path. Don't be fooled into believing that it's easy or you need luck to succeed. Your path will take you through valleys and up mountains. There will be victories, and there will be losses. People will come, and others will go. But if you continue to run your race, you will succeed, and it will be worth every heartache.

When your destiny begins to manifest, it will amaze you.

However, it will be awhile before you get there. This is a good thing. There are many levels that you must traverse to reach your destiny. As discussed in previous chapters, each level has its lessons that you must learn to be able to graduate to the next level. Fail the lesson; you fail the level. You will repeat the same lesson over again until you have mastered the lesson.

The purpose of a long, arduous road is to prepare you for your destiny. If you are not prepared for your destiny, you will lose it. Preparation is the key to obtaining success, but more importantly, it teaches you how to keep it. When things come easy, it makes it hard to value them. In contrast, when things come difficulty, you will fight to keep it. If it took you years to attain, you would make sure you don't lose it in seconds.

According to Time Magazine, 70% of people that get a sudden windfall of cash, like the lottery, will end up bankrupt in a few years. This happens to many athletes that come from disadvantaged backgrounds too. Handling success is a necessary and acquired skill. There is wisdom that can only be earned over time.

Storytime: Learning Value the Hard Way

I can attest in my own life how I lost many things because I was not prepared to handle them. At the time I lost them, I didn't even realize how valuable they were. It wasn't much time later when I tried to regain those things that I realized that what I was given was a gift. Because I didn't earn it the hard way, I didn't value it like I should have. Regaining what I lost was much harder the second, third, or fourth time. Each time became more difficult. But until I learned the lesson, I was doomed to repeat the mistake.

There were things in my own character that I needed to remove. One issue that I had was, I was habitually late to everything. This was bad because I didn't value time or being on time. At one job that I had I lived 5 minutes away and needed to be at work at 2 P.M., I wouldn't leave my house until 2 P.M. I abused the 7-minute grace period. I had many other jobs similar to that. I wouldn't leave home until the last minute and skate in just a few minutes late.

Doing so always left me unprepared and unprofessional. I always planned on just being on time rather than being early. Honestly, I couldn't see how being late could be seen as disrespectful. When you are late, you are telling the person waiting on you that you don't value them enough to be on time. It took me years to realize that.

I was always a very hard worker but was always late to work. I thought just my work ethic alone would allow me to get into management. I didn't see how this could affect my future opportunities. It wasn't until it was time for me to leave my job and pursue my business full-time. No longer would I be punching in a few minutes late. If I were late for a client, I would miss out on a contract.

To overcome this, I had to begin getting to work extremely early. At first, it was rough changing my routine to get prepared earlier than usual. I couldn't risk being on time, so I would get to work 1–3 hours ahead of my shift. I utilized the time to work on my business stuff until it was time to clock-in. I could not become a successful entrepreneur without learning to respect this fundamental principle. My last job was the final opportunity to learn the lesson, or it was going to directly affect my company reputation.

This chapter is meant to prepare you for the road ahead of you. Many success books don't speak much how hard the path will be. The publisher figures it would not be a very encouraging book if they spoke the truth. But, unless I am truthful, I will be doing you a disservice.

Many times this is why many people start, and then quit. They feel that they were lied to. No one told them how dark the nights really get. No one told them about how often your back will be against the wall during this journey. No one told them that when you step out of your comfort zone, you will get punched right in the nose by life.

Well, I am telling you. It is hard, but you will make it. I will share with you what is necessary to persevere on the road to your truth.

As you prepare your path, there are bad characteristics that you need to remove. And there are positive characteristics that need to be developed. Every negative and positive thing on the path holds a lesson. You have to pay attention to the lesson being taught and not what is actually happening to you.

The bad that comes is only the means of the lesson. Focusing on the situation will blind you from the lesson.

Roadwork

The sport I admire the most is boxing. Though I don't box, everything about the sport intrigues me. Most people that don't like boxing see it as a savage sport. Of this group, most have never attempted to try boxing or understand the sport. It is a very technical and strategic sport. Most would know from just watching it on television. I encourage anyone to take a few lessons to learn.

There are many nuances that go into throwing a punch. Without getting too complicated, there are many different types of punches and many different ways to defend a punch. To be effective, it's necessary to throw the right punch at the right time.

Likewise, you must defend the right punch at the right time or risk getting knocked out. It takes a lot of training to prepare to throw a punch. Yet, there is even more training that goes into preparing to fight in a match.

What I admire most about the sport is the preparation necessary to throw effective punches for 12 rounds fighting. The focus and determination necessary to prepare for a fight is unmatched by any non-combat sport. A fighter can spend several months preparing for one opponent. This consists of several hours of training every day until the day of the fight. They hit the punching bag, speed bag, sparring or practice fighting against an opponent, resistance training, abdominal training, and roadwork.

Roadwork shouldn't be confused with jogging. Jogging is an endurance exercise that consists of running forward in a linear or straight fashion. This type of training wouldn't work inside a ring in a fight. Fighting is much more dynamic. A boxer is usually moving from side-to-side, forwards, backwards, ducking, and dodging all while throwing punches at their adversary. A boxer must simulate this dynamic movement during training. Thus, roadwork is a combination of running, sprinting, side-to-side, forward, backward, ducking, dodging, and punching moves for miles at a time. This takes tremendous endurance.

Preparing for a fight in this manner is necessary to simulate the intensity of a fight. For many miles, a fighter is fighting an external battle and internal one. They are usually isolated during this part of training. Their coach isn't there with them during the miles of their feet hitting the pavement during their external battle. More importantly, they must overcome the internal battle of doubt, fear, fatigue. They're out there by themselves, giving and taking internal and external punches. It's a fight daily for several months.

As a result, on the day of the fight, they are both prepared mentally and physically for anything that may occur in the ring.

Your Roadwork

Fighters endure the arduous road to their ultimate fight by simulating fights and training mentally and physically for whatever may happen in the ring. Essentially, during practice, they are fighting unseen opponents daily throughout the days, weeks, and months leading up to the fight. The fight is just one night, while the training is several accumulated hours. This is why a fighter seems so confident before a fight. In their minds, they have already fought and defeated the opponent thousands of times. Mentally, they have already taken every punch of the opponent. And they have seen their own victory by knockout.

The same is true for your path towards your truth. You will be fighting both internal and external battles on your road. Your roadwork is practice for your fight the ultimate fight. It's to prepare you for graduating to your next level. Each level is guarded by your adversary. It's true that anything of value is always guarded. And your enemy doesn't want you to realize your true potential.

Your future is guarded by your adversary utilizing a network of opponents. They work as a coordinated team to keep you in your comfort zone. At each level, there are many layers of protection used by your enemy. Each layer is guarded by a different opponent, each with a goal of discouraging you long enough for you to give up hope and quit. They do not have the power to prevent your destiny, but they can wrestle with you long enough to get you off track. You have to decide to stop, but they can't make you stop.

Each enemy has a different strategy to defeat you. Yet, each enemy also requires a different strategy for you to beat them. The battle will be bloody, but the lesson and experience you will be left with will be valuable. The fight will change you for the better. It will strengthen your character, your faith and resolve.

As a result, you will become the person in your vision. Each battle brings you closer to your future success-self. Each battle leaves a little bit of the old you on the battlefield. Consequently, you grow and improve through each battle.

Growing into your destiny requires that you overcome each challenge you face. Your story only becomes a testimony that there was a test. Everyone has problems. But no one wants to hear the story of someone who never had troubles. There is no encouragement in that. Therefore, endure because your struggle is your testimony.

To give others hope, you must have triumphed over some obstacle. To build their faith, you must victoriously transition from one challenge to the next. To encourage others, you must have successfully gone through what others are currently dealing with.

This chapter is going to mentally prepare you for what's ahead. Be prepared to face your largest opponent at each stage of your journey. The bigger the prize at that level, the bigger the enemy guarding it. Let's start out with your initial stage. This is where we all start, but few actually transition out of.

Your Comfort Zone: Complacency

Complacency is the ruler of the comfort zone. Its intention is to keep you suspended in a realm of mediocrity. The is no growth in this land. Rather than focusing on improving, the people of this kingdom are focused on others. The culture of this domain is to surround yourself with unaspiring people that don't challenge you to be better. By surrounding yourself with unambitious people, it distracts you from changing your own situation.

The only way out your comfort zone is to confront fear. Fear must be overcome at every stage in life. But the first encounter with fear to leave your comfort zone is usually the worst. Fear causes inertia. Inertia is the tendency to do nothing or remain unchanged. Fear is subtle, but it can be identified through the lack of results. Results are hidden within opportunities.

The thing with opportunity is that it is usually mistaken for fear. There is always an opportunity to leave one level and transition to the next. However, people focus on fear instead of faith. They only focus on what can negatively happen and not the positive possibilities. This keeps people trapped in their comfort zone.

The only way to defeat fear is through faith. Faith is an action word. Therefore, defeating fear must be through action. Whatever you fear doing must be done. You cannot work around the enemy of fear; you must attack it head-on.

What you will face on your path to truth and destiny will push you past your perceived limits. You will have to see yourself and your situation differently if you plan on overcoming them. Looking at a new situation with old vision is a recipe for disaster. If you see things differently, you will act differently. Many fail on their path towards fulfillment because they refuse to grow in this way. They refuse to see things differently. They refuse to change their behavior for goal attainment. They would rather be miserable and comfortable than driven and fulfilled.

You will face Giants, Storms, and Mountains on your path. Do not turn from these challenges. They are not meant to harm you but to help you. Recognize that no weapon formed against you will prosper. The weapons of the enemy are meant for your good. They are tools of preparation for your journey and goal attainment.

Begin by seeing your challenges differently. If you begin seeing your situations differently, they will start changing right before your eyes. There is a lesson and purpose to everything in your path. Rather than complaining and remaining in your problem, begin looking for what you are supposed to be learning as a result. Complaining will leave you in your problem. Changing your perception will be the only way out.

Giants on Your Path

Embarking on your journey outside of your comfort zone will entail many battles. The first are giants that you must overcome. You can consider giants as Gatekeepers to your next level. For example, starting a business, going back to school, or writing your first book. Giants are big and scary but on the other side of your giant is a promotion.

As mentioned before, everything of value is guarded. Every blessing has a price, but so few are willing to pay it. The bigger the giant on your path, the bigger the blessing. Therefore, giants should be viewed as doorways to your next opportunity for promotion. But because they are big and scary, most people see them as impossibilities. But, how can someone like me with no experience or education accomplish something like that? This thinking allows doubt and fear to keep them bonded in their current dimension. They never face their giants, and remain living an underwhelming life full of regrets.

Essentially, the giants are road markers on your path directing you to your truth. Elevating to the next level is through adversity. By not turning down the path to face your giant, you are forfeiting your destiny. You are also putting the lives and destinies of others at risk. There is no way around your giant; you have to go through them.

Overcoming each giant needs a different strategy. The giant you faced in your past is not the same one in your present. Hence, you cannot defeat a new giant with the same strategy. You must be attuned to the situation to discover your approach for victory. Your victory is determined by the action you take. The wrong action will always yield you the wrong result. Likewise, the lack of action will produce no results. Thus, entering into each conflict with your giant requires execution of certain actions at the perfect time for victory.

Any missteps will cause you to fail. Any missed lessons will cause failure too. You may have to face the same giant over again until you learn how to win. There may be an undeveloped skill you must master to defeat it. For example, you may have to learn better how to manage your finances, to study better, or to better proofread your written work. The more you improve, the more effective your attacks against your giant become. And then it is only a matter of time before your giant falls.

No half-hearted efforts will defeat your opponent. Giants do fall if you wallop them enough. This will take full-faith, full-effort, and accuracy to bring them down. Be ready to fight every day until your giant comes crashing down.

Success is on the other side of your giant. You cannot be too fearful to engage your giant. Be courageous, tenacious, and willing to learn if you plan on conquering your opportunity for promotion. Be warned: just because it is your destiny doesn't mean it will be easy. It just means that you are guaranteed a victory if you don't quit. Stay in the fight until you win.

Storms on Your Path

There is a saying, which I have heard from an older generation, "If you live long enough, you will encounter a storm."

Storms are an inevitable part of life. There is no way you can avoid them; you're guaranteed to encounter one. You are either coming out of one, entering one, or in one. But, it's up to you if you come out of your storms.

Storms are good for developing into your full potential. They build toughness, resolve, and faith. Without storms, we cannot fully develop the weak areas in our character. Without storms, we cannot fulfill our assignment in our next season. The purpose of your storm is to stretch your abilities by causing you to focus on a multitude of things at once. In a storm, you can't just focus on one thing at a time. Storms force you to juggle many things at once without them crashing to the ground.

Essentially, I would describe a storm as a set of problems you will encounter on your journey. Some storms are bigger than others. Some storms are even more violent than others. They are very similar to the natural storms that occur in nature. The strength of the storms is seen in the winds, rain, and lightning. Natural storms and the storms of life have the power to uproot whatever is in its way. If you are not secure in your faith, truth, and path, you will find yourself blown around by the storms of life.

An example of a storm would be: You're working full-time and considered going back to school to get your degree. A several weeks after the semester begins, you have a parent that becomes hospitalized with an illness. You are too far into the semester to quit without penalty, and you have exams and assignments that are due in a few weeks. Now you have a decision to make. Do you quit school and focus on your parent? Or do you learn how to juggle until the semester ends?

Most people quit to end up never going back to school. The ones that choose to remain in school find a way to finish the semester. This is in spite of working full-time, taking care of the family at home, tending to an ill parent, studying and getting assignments done. They stretch their capacity to do more. As a result, they can receive more in return.

This is not the easiest way to get to your goals, but the experience grows you for the better. Stretching hurts during the process, but you get used to it. What was once difficult becomes your new normal.

You must remain on your path while braving your storm. If you choose to only engage your storm, you will forfeit your path. But if you remain in the struggle and push through your storm, you will prove your truth to yourself. Your next level requires you to be able to do more. Because you've expanded your capacity, you are qualified to matriculate to the next level.

Mountains on Your Path

Mountains are catastrophic challenges that arise on your path to truth. What makes mountains different from your storms is that there are no obvious solutions to the problems. It's impossible for you to fix yourself. You would need a miracle to move the mountain. You must face your impossibility because just ignoring your mountain won't make it disappear.

Every challenge on your path has a purpose. Every giant is meant to reveal your opportunities for promotion. Every storm is meant to stretch your abilities and increase your capacity. Your mountain is meant to test you. Your mountain will test if you truly believe in your truth. The best way to prove your truth is to test it against the impossible. Can you walk your path with no visible sign there will be a finish line?

Yes, you must walk forward. I can confidently tell you that your mountain will bring forth the most compelling testimony.

Regardless of your circumstance, even against impossibility, your truth will still stand.

Know that the fiercer the trial, the larger the reward. Take comfort that there is a great prize on the other side of the mountain. Don't expect it to be easy, but expect it to be worth it. However, know that you must outlast the mountain to attain your prize.

Mountains can't stop you, but they can discourage you from fulfilling your assignment. Standing in the shadow of your mountain, your truth seems like a dead end. Your mountain may be a bad doctor's report, a debt letter from your mortgage company, or the possibility of having to close your business. Fearing your mountain will keep you trapped in your valley. But through facing your mountain, you'll learn to surmount it.

During this trial, you will learn what you are really made of. The mountain will test your faith, truth, and resolve. Can you stay resolute when tasked with the impossible? Can you find hope where there is none? Will you persevere through this process? The successful do. The successful find a way. To find your own success in this situation, you have to make up your mind that you will not turn back. Remain resolute, regardless of how big a shadow your mountain is casting on you.

Believing that you will triumph must be seen in your action. Those that doubt don't act. But those who believe walk out their faith. Your faith must be evident in your daily action. This is easier said than done. However, to do so, you must first guard your mind of doubt. Secondly, you must discipline yourself from speaking doubt. And lastly, you must focus on your daily tasks to bring down your mountain.

By doing so, you are taking your focus off of the size of the mountain and keeping it fixed on your destiny. Your mountain is large and intimidating; however, you can change the size of your mountain by the way you view it. Perception is everything. Impossibilities and possibilities only occur in your mind. You must see yourself achieving your goal every day. In the natural, you will see your mountain daily. But in your mind, you must see yourself prevailing.

Nothing is impossible for those who believe. But everything is impossible for those who doubt. Without belief, it's impossible to overcome your mountain. Without your faith in action, your mountain will never be moved.

At the end, whatever is left standing up wins. Mountains don't last forever. You can outlast it if you believe you can. Your belief will inspire belief in others. But without a test, there can be no testimony. You can't build someone else up unless you have been torn down yourself but overcame. Your story of endurance will encourage others. You will build their faith to endure their mountains if you remain steadfast on your path.

Chapter 7: Quotes to Live by Your Path

"You are only confined to the walls you build yourself"-
Anonymous

"For every path you choose there is one you must abandon, usually forever. " -- Joan D. Vinge

"There are some things that you can only learn from a storm"-- Joel Osteen

"Hardships often prepare ordinary people for extraordinary destinies"-- C. S. Lewis

"For we walk by faith and not by sight." – 2 Corinthians 5:7

FINISH

Chapter 8:
Your Breakthrough

Throughout the book, you have seen how your mind plays the largest part in your victory. For breakthrough to occur in your life, it must happen internally first. Unless it happens within it won't happen without.

Breakthrough isn't a destination or a manifestation of a long-awaited reward. It is the awakening, awareness, revelation in mind of an overcomer. Regardless, what stands in their way they know they will have the victory. It has been proven to you that no weapon is able to prosper against you. The enemy will form the weapon, used it, but you prevailed.

It amazes me how soldiers are trained to run towards gunfire. This is done mostly in boot camp training and experience in battle. The boot camp training teaches the soldier to fight by means of intense battle simulation. As a result, they are able to strategically think and execute plans while bullets are flying by their heads. Through training, they are trained to follow orders in the face of any opposition. Boot camp instills the trust in their training and not in their emotions.

Similarly, the boot camp training of this book was the first several chapters. In them, I explained what you should expect during your training/path towards your truth. Each chapter introduced you to your enemy and warned you of his tactics. To respond to this reviewed your own counter-attack strategy for your enemy, giants, storms, and mountains.

The previous chapters stressed how important having the right team around you was. And the impact a wrong team will have on your destiny. As far as growing into your truth, you read how personal development plays a key role in your growth and success. Moreover, without the development of your strengths and weaknesses, you are vulnerable to attack from your enemy.

Now, you have the mindset, weapons, and relationships that will ensure success. This chapter is about the expectations of a breakthrough. What can you expect as a result of your changed mindset? What does success really look like? And how to handle the status changes as you elevate.

Always Breaking Through

Through your training, you understand that breakthrough only occurs in your reality when first you've lived it in your mind. Any type of external change without an internal change will only last temporarily. For lasting change, it must first come from within.

This enduring mentality is necessary because you will always need to breakthrough something. You will always face opposition as you're in your purpose. You are either in a problem, coming out of a problem, or about to enter a problem. There is no escaping problems and issues. They are as much a part of your path as you are. Thus, the reason your mindset must be steadfast.

The funny thing is that some people believe that staying in their comfort zone exempts them from problems. There are problems there too. But, the problems in your comfort zone are meant to motivate you out. But, most people take it as a sign to stay in. This is similar to a mother eagle who stirs up her nest to motivate her babies to leave.

When the birds are at flying age, the mother eagle begins pulling up the soft, feathery flooring of the nest uncovering the pointy branches and jagged rocks beneath. The mother eagle will also shake the nest and begin feeding her maturing eagles less to further motivate. For flight training, she will drop the baby eagles them from tremendous heights to exercise their flying muscle as they the feverishly flap their wings. She will catch them before are close to hitting anything hard. But then she just flies even higher to repeat this process.

This may sound mean, but this is for the maturing of the eagles. They will never leave the nest otherwise. Because complacency is a destroyer. The mother eagle understands that she will not always be there to fend for them they must learn to fend for themselves. Hence, the difficulties she creates is only for their good. By stirring the nest, she is motivating them to grow into mature eagles.

Equally, the trials you go through are for your maturing. They aren't meant to harm you but move you into your full potential. It's unlikely that we would move out of our comfort zones without motivation. But without growth, there is only death. It's a part of nature. Things that refuse to grow in nature will soon die. The leaf that refuses to grow to get the most sunlight will soon be overshadowed by leaves that grow. Before you know it the leaf withers away.

The same is true for you. The areas of your life you refuse to focus and grow will wither away. That is why we have giants for new opportunities. Storms to shift our focus. And mountains to cultivate maturity. Without problems, we cease being fruitful. Thus, the problems will never stop. Understand that it part of the process.

Your Changed Mind

Similar to a soldier, you have successfully gone through training the way you react to trials in your life have changed.

You can no longer react emotionally to everything that occurs to you. Though is impossible to be emotionless we must learn to control our emotions. As a result, you no longer think the worse of our situations. Fear only occurs in the mind. That is the only place it can exist and flourish if you allow. As you are focusing on fear, you're not focused on solutions.

The only way out of any difficulty is the one we create. We are only able to create when we are focused. Our time, energy, and focus is limited therefore wasting it on fear only drains us. Only when we are focused on coming out of our valleys can we create a plan out.

Fear keeps us focus on defeat. Whatever you focus on will magnify in our minds. Eventually, it will manifest in our realities. This is why staying positive during difficulties is so important. What you fear will show up. Likewise, what you faith will show up too.

Therefore, you cannot walk your path being fearful of your next move. Trust that your next move is the right one through faith. Doing so will allow you to capitalize on opportunities. Hesitation will only lead to your own failure.

Since our time is limited, timing is essential to success. Opportunities only occur in small windows of time. Not reacting soon enough can be detrimental. Moving too quick can be harmful too. Knowing when to act too quick at the right time takes discernment. Without a discerning spirit, you will miss countless windows of opportunities.

Develop your discernment by staying aligned with your truth throughout your journey. The spirit is similar to your intuition. It will guide you along your path. It will tell you when to move, who to speak to, and to who to avoid. You are only able to hear this inner spirit by staying focused on your truth. When you are distracted by fear, it becomes difficult to hear your inner guiding spirit. Keep your mind clear of doubt and listen intently for instruction.

With discernment you can move about and capitalize on situations others won't see. You will be a step ahead of your competition. You will know the next move of your enemy before he does. This allows you to position yourself at the right place, at the right time, with the right strategy.

The tendency of a breakthrough mindset is to be single-minded on victory. Nothing can distract you from it. No giant, storm or mountain can stand in your way. As soon as they appear you are seeking discernment for victory. Focusing on action keeps you feeling the pressure of the situation. Even though the fiery darts of your enemy is flying by your head, your mind is shielded by faith.

What Success Really Looks Like

There is a misconception of what success really looks like. People imagine success to be having a cool drink on a hot beach. No worries or cares in the world. Many people envy the

Successful-Few because they believe that they don't have any issues in life. This couldn't be further from the truth. In reality, the more successful you are, the more issues you have to deal with.

Why is this true? Though you might be wealthy, healthy, and happy, most of the people you deal with are not. Many people want what you have. But, they don't want to endure what you had to get it. Somehow, they feel entitled to what you earned. As a result, you may encounter few people who will lie, cheat, and steal to take what is rightfully yours. Therefore, you will need to spend some of your time defending what have.

Contrary to what you may think, people like Bill Gates, Oprah, Sir Richard Branson, or Warren Buffet spend parts of their days defending their castles even though they could be enjoying the rest of their lives on a private beach somewhere. Why don't they? They love what they do. Therefore, they spend most of their days doing what is required of them so they can do what they love. What they are passionate about is not found on a hot beach. What they love is fulfilling their purpose on this earth by helping others.

The successful spend countless of business meetings all day so they can impact the lives of others through other endeavors. The successful fight countless lawsuits all day so they can change the lives of the less fortunate around the world. The successful do what is not glamorous so that others can benefit. To them, the good always outweighs the bad.

Thus, success really looks like more work. But the work gives the less fortunate food, necessary medicine and surgeries, and housing. So, they will always trade settling out of court to avoid long, drawn-out lawsuits so you can focus on what's important. They endure so others can be blessed through their efforts.

However, it's not all work. Being successful has its perks.

You do get to enjoy your cool drink on a hot beach sometimes. But you don't remain on vacation. What draws you back to reality is purpose. You are destined to be a blessing. You have the power to help so many people. Don't take it for granted. Be willing to work. This is the only way you benefit the lives of the less fortunate.

Your success has a more immediate impact too. Because you endure you're able to help your loved ones too. You're able to enrich their lives through different experiences and more time spent together. This couldn't be afforded to you without the willingness to work.

In addition, with success, there is the power of discretionary time. Being able to dictate your calendar is your biggest benefit. Deciding when you get to spend time with loved ones and for how long is true power. This power brings happiness. Time is a limited resource you don't want to spend it on things that don't bring you joy.

Handling Your Status Change

Like I mentioned above, work ethic is necessary to maintain success. In addition, maintaining a humble attitude will always preserve your success.

Arrogance always comes before a fall. No one is immune to that. It's impossible for you to know everything. Therefore, you can learn from anyone if you're wise enough to listen.

Furthermore, being successful in one arena doesn't make you successful in all arenas. Michael Jordan is arguably one of the greatest basketball players to every play. But when he transitioned to playing baseball in the early 1990s he was barely good enough to play professional baseball.

Michael grew up playing baseball and basketball in North Carolina. But once he got to high school he chose to stick with basketball. Since then he devoted all of his time to improving in basketball and became a legend as a result. This all changed when he decided to play baseball. He was no longer the best on the planet. He was below average. After one season of playing Minor League baseball, he returned to basketball.

Even legends aren't great in everything. As you become more successful, you need to fight to remain humble. It is easy to become arrogant. You begin believing what others say about your greatness. You become arrogant when you believe you have arrived. You stop learning and growing. When you are not growing, you are slowly withering away.

To avoid this stay hungry. Be concerned with getting better. Continually focus on getting better through the development of your talents, skills, gifts and knowledge. Be willing to learn from others. Read more, experience more, listen more and you will have more.

And lastly, you must also learn what to say no to. It is totally fine to not be able to do everything you were once able to do with those you were once able to do it with. Your time is much more valuable now. Spend it with those that value it the most.

Time spent doing what you must do for work will take up a lot of your time. The time left over is limited. Utilize it well. Spend time with loved ones. More importantly, spend time recharging yourself. You give plenty out. But not replacing it is unwise. You will burn out. You can get unhappy even doing what you love. Practice self-care to recharge your energy, focus, and passion.

A Walking Testimony

As you traverse through different seasons in your life, you will encounter trials and tribulations. Each is more intense than the last. Each with a purpose to prepare you for the next level.

Some of the trials will knock you down. But, you'll get back up. At some points in your journey, it will seem like all your enemies are attacking you from all sides. But, if you remain in the fight you will eventually overcome.

Your story will be your testimony. A walking testimony is a public trial in your life. This is when everyone knows your "business". What you and your family are going through becomes very public. People are watching you lose everything. There may be false allegations against you. Your reputation will be damaged before the truth comes to light. Your relationships will be strained during and may never be the same after. All you have to stand on is the promise that you will win.

But, looking at your circumstance, it looks very bleak. These situations make it very hard for you to even be yourself. You can lose faith. You can lose joy. You can even lose the hope that this trial will turn out for your good.

But it will...

A walking testimony is a walking believer. They don't remain in their valley. They take steps every day to walk out. As your trial was public so will be your victory.

But what is most important is the walking. The daily process of you doing what you say you believe. Even though your faith, joy, and hope are waning you continue walking. While others are laughing, you are walking. While others are being critical, you are walking. While the odds seem insurmountable, you remain walking.

One foot in front of the other through your process. One step at a time through your valley. You may be surrounded by mountains, but one day you will walk into green pastures. Seasons must change. But you must keep walking.

Everyone loves a comeback story. The reason why is that they remind them of their own possibilities. While people are watching you walk through your valley, you are giving them hope. If you made it, they can too. Your testimony is meant to empower. But unless you walk through your valley there can be no witnesses to your victory. People need to see you overcome. They need to witness the authenticity of your truth.

Enjoying the Process

With our eyes so fixed on the destination, we can lose sight enjoying our journey. Realizing breakthrough is a process. It is difficult and takes time. Unless you are finding joy in your journey your life will be full of accomplishments but void of love and happiness.

Life is too short for it not to be enjoyed. You should take time out to take pleasure in the little things in life. This is called being present.

In a world of multitasking, we are rewarded for being able to do many things at once. Some people are more talented in others in this area. But we all try to do or best version of multitasking. We are driving and on the phone. We are answering text messages and half-listen to the people in front of us. We are watching a movie with family but checking out status updates social media.

We are becoming more distracted. We are too busy trying to get things done but miss what is directly in front of us. Every day is a gift. But we treat as such. We act as if today is getting in the way of our destiny. We rush through our day to get to the next. We become high-stressed, sleep deprived, and over-stimulated.

Personally, I have been guilty of this. When I was first was working in my business full-time I would be working 16-hour days. I was always working. Even when I was with clients, I would try to get other work done too. It was pretty bad.

Even the little time I spent with my family seemed like an annoyance to me. I was constantly on my phone missing the precious minutes with my loved ones. I had a tough time turning this intense focus off. But, my wife had to bring me back to reality. I was working so hard for her, but then I was losing her at the same time. She didn't want my business but wanted me. I wanted my business, her, then my health in that order. You can't have it all at once. I needed to prioritize to remain present.

Eventually, I learned to shut it down once I got home. I would put my phone in the bedroom and spend time with my family in the living room. It was tough but necessary. Now, it is much easier and really look forward to spending time with loved ones as much as possible.

There is so much more in our day that we are not taking advantage of. You must ask yourself "At the end of the day what is most important?" This is the fruitful relationships with our loved ones. No amount of success can compare.

I'm not saying that fulfilling your truth is not important, but it is not the only important aspect of life. You should maximize your potential. You should fulfill your destiny. But if you plan to enjoy the journey towards it, you have to find time to slow down and be present.

You can either have a house full of trophies or a home full of love. You have to decide on the most important things. And put your effort into maintaining that decision. This is the greatest balancing act of all time. Balancing your purpose to the world and your purpose to your loved ones.

You will have to set boundaries with yourself, purpose and loved ones. And have family hold you accountable to them.

Learn to make sacrifices for your loved ones not in spite of them. Sleep a little less to get your day started earlier. Plan your schedule with family first then filling in the rest.

Learn to divide your time wisely between your family, purpose, and yourself. Take time out for yourself so you can be your best when you're with them. Likewise, you can't be your best-self to others of you're not your best-self to yourself.

There is time for everything if you manage your time well. You cannot get everything accomplished in one your day. But don't let that ruin your day. Stop and smell the flowers occasionally. Your journey will be much more enjoyable with the love of others to keep you.

Your Breakthrough Manifested

Now you are at the final stage of the process. It is time for the physical manifestation of your breakthrough. It is long-awaited, and you have endured many sleepless nights for it. But it's worth it.

You have walked the breakthrough process of preparation, expectation, and manifestation. Your path was meant to prepare you to not only obtain and sustain your breakthrough. The preparation process was to change your mindset. The changed mindset changed your perception, and you were able to see that breakthrough was possible for you. This gave you hope. Eventually, your hope grew to faith. Then your faith grew into expectation. Now, it's no longer a possibility but an assurance.

Expectation is the essential ingredient to manifestation. You can walk your path and doubt and receive nothing as a result. Or you can believe and expect your physical breakthrough to manifest. Without the middle step can be no breakthrough.

I liken the breakthrough process to giving birth. The first 9-months are preparation stage. This portion is to prepare the parents for the baby. The parents buy the tools necessary to care for the child once it arrives. They paint the child's room, buy diapers and toys.

Then there is the expectation stage when the water breaks. At this point it's no longer a possibility but an assurance that the baby is coming. The contractions begin and the body begins the birthing process. The pain increases as it gets closer to the birth. Regardless of how much pain the mother is in, they are asked to push their baby out.

This brings us to the final stage of manifestation. The mother pushes with each contraction moves the baby closer to the birth canal. The top of the baby's head begins to show, but it's not time to stop. The mother must continue pushing through the pain, through the fatigue, and emotions until the baby's head is completely out. They push until their breakthrough is fully manifested.

At this stage is no longer a dream or possibility but reality. There is no denying your Breakthrough. It's here. Its presence is proof that you walked the process of your truth until it became reality. You continued to move forward regardless of the obstacles that were in your way. You continued forward when others deserted you. You continued forward until you got breakthrough.

Notice that through the birthing process that it was most difficult right before the breakthrough. Take note that the pain increases the closer one gets to realizing their truth. Make a note to remember that when the baby begins crowning, you must still push through until you have breakthrough.

The pain will be a sign that you are close to your Breakthrough. Some people quit at this point and go through the process in vain. They quit just moments away from what they have been praying, crying and believing for.

Don't quit like the infamous gold minor that stopped just a few feet from gold. It is right there for you if you keep moving forward. Get your reward for the pain during preparation. Reach for what was destined to be yours. You have paid the price now it's time to capture it.

Chapter 8: Quotes to Live by Your Breakthrough

"The pain you have been feeling can't compare to the joy that is coming." —Romans 8:18

"We don't grow when things are easy; we grow when we face challenges." —Anonymous

"Breakthroughs occur when limiting thoughts and behaviors are challenged." —Fabienne Fredrickson

"When you are tempted to give up, your breakthrough is right around the corner." —Joyce Meyer

"Sometimes it takes an overwhelming breakdown to have an undeniable breakthrough." —Anonymous

About the Author

Gladimir Simeon
Business and Life Empowerment Coach

You <u>know</u> you have it in you to change.
But do you <u>believe</u> you can change?
Gladimir "Coach Glad" Simeon is an experienced entrepreneur, dynamic speaker and empowering coach who educates and empowers his diverse clientele to conquer business and personal challenges.

Glad goes beyond the tips and quick-fix gimmicks seen in the media and understands that to achieve success in all areas of life, mental hurdles must first be overcome.

Through his knowledgeable, humorous and intuitive approach, negative thinking is redirected into positive thinking. It is one thing to know, but it is another to believe you have it in you to change. Harness your internal strength to transform your external circumstances.

Gladimir Simeon earned his Bachelor of Science degree in Exercise Science and Health Promotion from Florida Atlantic University in the hope of enriching people's lives through wellness.

He and his wife own and operate Glad Health & Fitness, Inc.; Glad Health Transport, Inc.; The Simeon Group Publishing,

Inc.; and Coach Glad, Inc., all with the purpose of allowing people to live their lives to the fullest through their unique products and services.

A Call to Purpose

Gladimir always felt that he was called for more even though his environment and circumstances said differently. This left him frustrated, overweight, and depressed. It wasn't until he stepped out of his comfort to discover his purpose that he found happiness. He began to unearth who he was and what he was truly meant to be. The journey of self-discovery gave him great joy, and he desired that others "grow" through the same experience.

Now Glad has been impacting the lives of others through business, wellness, and life. He encourages others to pursue their greatness by pushing past any perceived boundaries. In doing so, they would discover their true selves.

He feels that everyone was sent to earth with an assignment to fulfill. It won't happen in your comfort zone. His goal is to change the lives of others by helping them to take action on their dreams through personal development, inspiration, and action.

The journey won't be easy, but it will always be worth it.

-Be unstoppable

To Book for Speaking Please Contact:
www.coachglad.com
coachglad1@gmail.com
954-245-7911